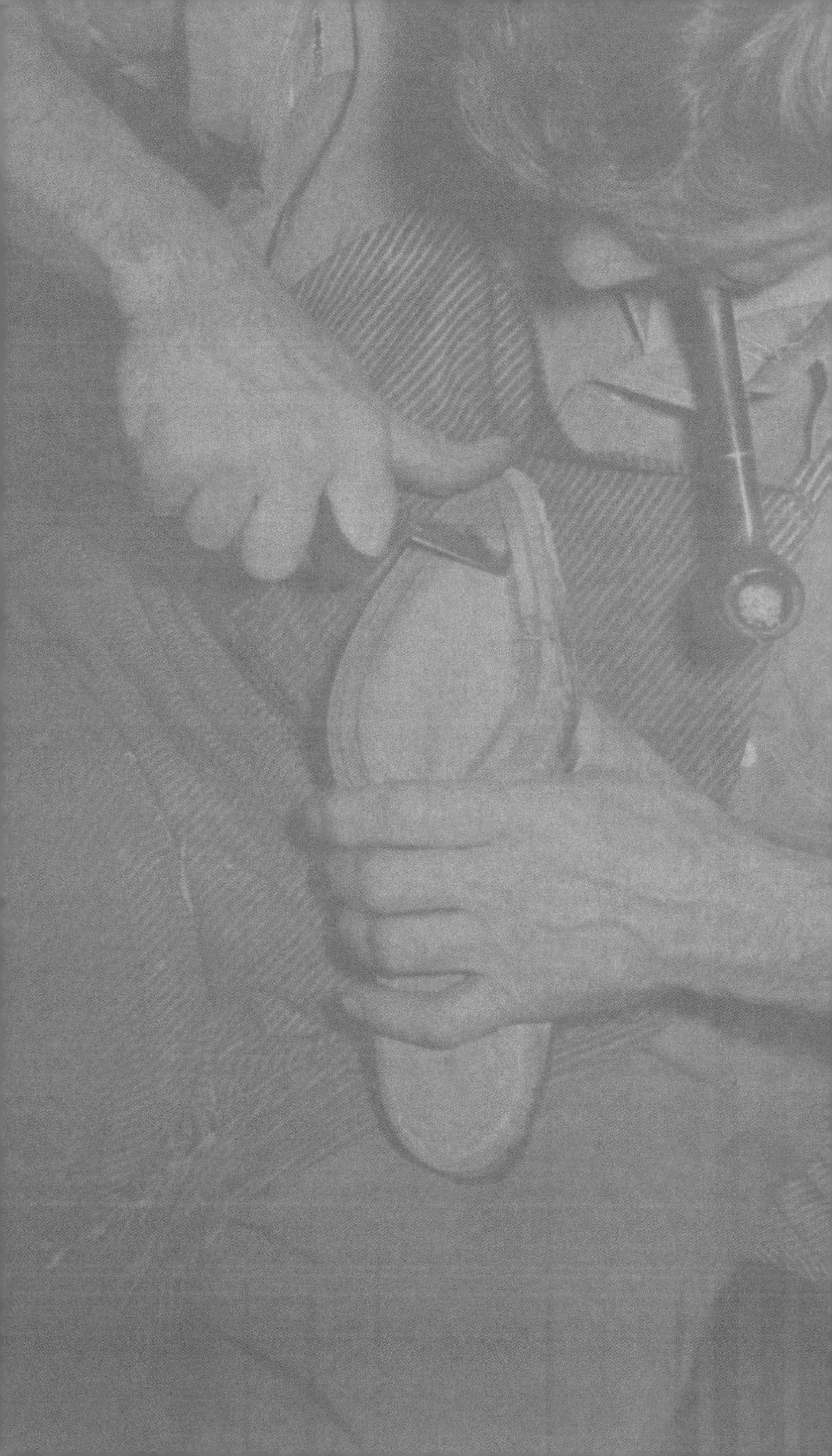

ROUGH AND READY

ROUGH AND READY

A HISTORY OF COWBOY BOOTS

Elizabeth Semmelhack

With contributions by Nishi Bassi, Lee Miller,
Jamie Nudie, Lisa Sorrell, and Justine Woods

Rizzoli Electa

The story of the cowboy boot—steeped in history and legend—is neither simple nor straightforward. Indeed, it is rife with paradoxes. Since their invention in the late nineteenth century, cowboy boots have symbolized labor and leisure, freedom and domination, violence and romance, as well as politics and identity. Cowboy boots were born out of industrialization but were refined through craftsmanship. They have served as emblems of individuality and, at the same time, instruments of cultural cohesion. They were central to the "closing" of the West, yet they remain enduring symbols of open skies and boundless freedom.

In grappling with these wide-ranging issues, this book does not present a simple timeline of boot design, nor does it function as a catalogue of makers. Instead, it asks how the cowboy came to be, what he came to symbolize, and how the stories told shaped the boots he wore. Tracing the boot's evolution from equestrian tool to fashion statement takes the reader through cattle drives and Wild West shows, into Hollywood fantasies and onto presidential podiums, revealing how boots both responded to and influenced changes in taste, politics, and culture.

The journey begins in chapter one, "Real," which uncovers the origins of the North American cowboy and the footwear that served him. The story starts with the Spaniards' invasion of Anáhuac (Mexico) and the cattle and horses they brought from Iberia and North Africa. Out of this violent collision of cultures, Indigenous knowledge of the land blended with Spanish and West African traditions of cattle management to shape cowboys' life and gear. By the era of the post–Civil War cattle drives, when cowboys were driving herds north to railheads, the cowboy boot began to take shape with the addition of high heels and decorative stitching. The chapter closes with Justine Woods's essay on the meaning of fringe in Western dress, reminding us that even seemingly ornamental details of cowboy attire carry deep cultural weight.

Performance takes center stage in chapter two, "Rodeo," which explores how spectacle helped shape the cowboy boot into the icon it is today. *Buffalo Bill's Wild West Show* and early cinema transformed the boot from practical gear into a cultural signifier, popularizing ever more decorative features. Boots began to reflect not only the demands of the range but also the shifting trends of fashion. The chapter concludes with an interview with famed bespoke cowboy boot maker Lee Miller, whose reflections on skill, tradition, and innovation bridge the past with the present.

From performance the story moves into spectacle. Chapter three, "Rhinestone," follows the rise of the singing cowboy and the impact of country-and-western music in the 1930s through the 1950s. Hollywood and radio made stars out of Gene Autry and Roy Rogers, who dazzled in brightly decorated boots. Boot makers responded with vivid inlays, sparkling embellishments, and intricate designs that turned footwear into flamboyant stagecraft. This chapter ends with an interview with Jamie Nudie, granddaughter of famed rodeo tailor Nudie Cohn, who recalls her family's role in defining this glittering era.

The paradox of authenticity returns in chapter four, "Right," which traces the postwar fixation on "true grit" and hardworking boots. In popular culture and politics, boots became shorthand for toughness, independence, and moral clarity. Presidents donned them to broadcast rugged individualism, while films vacillated between nostalgic Westerns and darker reinterpretations of the genre. Yet even as plain working boots carried connotations of courage, the 1980s saw a revived interest in cowboy boot ornamentation that ushered in a new golden age of bootmaking at the end of the century. The chapter concludes with Nishi Bassi's essay on Ralph Lauren, whose vision of Western dress shaped fashion far beyond the United States.

The story culminates in chapter five, "Reclaimed," which witnesses the cowboy boot being wrested back from the myths that long defined it and reinvented by a new generation of boot makers. This reclamation honors the diverse histories embedded in the history of the cowboy boot celebrated on the runways in Paris and in the nightclubs of Mexico. The chapter also looks at the surge in women becoming master boot makers. The final interview in the book is with Lisa Sorrell, whose reflections on her craft underscore how bootmaking is both a personal art form and a dialogue with history.

By closely examining the myriad stories of the cowboy boot, a greater appreciation of them and all their contradictions might emerge. Surely, the cowboy boot endures as a powerful symbol in America and around the world, not because it resolves these contradictions, but because it embodies them.

REAL

The story of the cowboy and his boots begins long before the arrival of Europeans in the Americas. Yet the boots and the culture that have come to define the cowboy are distinctly North American, profoundly shaped by modern forces from industrialization to mass media. Indeed, the cowboy boot is, in many ways, as much a product of Hollywood as it is of the historical West. Its evolution reflects a complex interplay of cultural and political forces: migration, economic transformation, nation building, and the persistent reinvention of the West. But it is also the story of skilled makers whose artistry and craftsmanship shaped one of America's most enduring icons.

COWBOY NECESSITIES

In order to be a cowboy, one needs cattle, land for grazing, a swift horse, and the responsibility of managing a herd. Long before the colonization of the Americas, many cultures across Europe, Asia, and Africa herded cattle on horseback, innovating tools that would go on to be central to the development of cowboy accoutrements in North America. Two of the most important were the stirrup and the heel.

The stirrup, in use by the fourth century in East Asia and by the sixth in Western Asia, revolutionized horseback riding by dramatically enhancing riders' stability.[1] The high heel, invented in Western Asia to complement the stirrup, gave riders even greater stability, which allowed them to wield larger weaponry (fig. 1).[2] When the Umayyad Caliphate invaded Iberia from North Africa in the early eighth century, they brought with them the stirrup, the North African Barbay horse, and a range of other material goods and practices that would impact cattle herding in Spain (fig. 2).[3]

The Iberian Peninsula had long been home to cattle, and the arid conditions of the Spanish highlands required open-range livestock management, with cattle roaming freely and rounded up only annually. The horses suited to the challenges of the open range were hardy Spanish Barbs, bred from North African and Iberian horses. This system would prove to work well in the similar landscapes of central and northern Mexico when the Spanish colonists began to raise cattle (fig. 3).

Fig. 1: This pair of Iranian riding shoes most likely dates to the 18th or early 19th century. Heels were worn in Iran from as early as the 10th century and were designed to secure the foot in the stirrup. Europeans adopted heels— a key innovation that would later influence cowboy boot design—at the turn of the 17th century.

NEW SPAIN

In the early days of the colonial project in "New Spain," as Mexico was called, the Spanish established the *encomienda* system, which granted land to colonial *encomenderos*, giving them the right to demand labor and/or tribute from the Indigenous inhabitants of that land. As the Indigenous populations declined due to violence and disease, ever larger tracts of land began to be given to colonists. Initially, these land grants were used to grow the food long cultivated by Indigenous farmers, but the expanding colonial presence also came with a demand for food similar to what had been enjoyed in Spain, including beef. The increasing value of cattle, combined with the expanding size of land grants, ultimately paved the way for large ranches, called haciendas. However, with only a relatively small Spanish colonial workforce available, a pressing question arose—who would perform the demanding, hands-on work of managing the cattle herds?

In Spain, vaqueros—"cow workers" —had long been low-paid laborers tasked with the job of herding cattle on horseback. In New Spain, Indigenous people, despite declining populations, were theoretically "available" for such work. However, the colonists feared that if Indigenous people learned to ride, they would resist or escape Spanish rule, so they were forbidden to do so. Instead, enslaved Africans—forcibly removed from their homelands, stripped of their networks, unfamiliar with the land, and subjected to extreme control measures—were forced into service. Many of the enslaved came from West Africa and had deep cultural traditions of horseback riding and cattle management—and they became the first cowboys of the Americas.

MOVING NORTH

The discovery of silver north of Mexico City in the mid-sixteenth century further increased the value of cattle, as the animals provided meat for the miners, tallow for the candles needed underground, and

Fig. 2: A Moorish horseman from *Cavaliers nègres, polonais et hongrois*. Stefano della Bella, c. 1651.

Fig. 3: Durán Codex. Diego Durán, c. 1581.

hides for the bags used to transport the extracted silver. As the cattle herds were pushed north, the semiarid landscape of the Central Mexican Plateau proved perfect for open-range herding. However, the region and the numerous Indigenous nations that lived there had never been a part of the Aztec Empire, and the incursion of colonial prospectors and land-hungry cattle owners, along with their indentured or enslaved Indigenous and African laborers, was met with fierce resistance.

In principle, the Spanish government included nominal protections for Indigenous land rights, but the discovery of silver saw the expansion of land grants given to Spanish elites and the increasing encroachment onto Indigenous lands. Cattle owners ruthlessly exploited the ambiguous definitions of "common land," and forcibly seized territory and subjugated Indigenous peoples, creating a new form of encomienda focused solely on labor.[4]

Not far behind these incursions came the Catholic missions, established under the guise of ministering to "pagan" populations—guiding them toward Christianity and offering protection. Yet once Indigenous nations were "pacified" and converted into "Mission Indians," they were forcibly put to work, tasked with providing food and other necessities for the missions. Conveniently, the missions were almost always located near places where labor was in high demand, such as mines and private ranches, encouraging further exploitation of Indigenous workers.[5]

VAQUEROS

As ranching expanded, so did the need for labor. By the second half of the sixteenth century, the law had been changed to allow some Indigenous people the right to ride.[6] In the outer reaches of the empire, the need for workers made following the law to the letter inconvenient. Thus, those who worked with cattle on horseback were composed of a range of fully enslaved or debt-bondage Africans, Indigenous people, and mestizos. As in Spain, these workers were called *vaqueros* and were fully embedded into the larger feudal-like colonial ranching network. Out on the arid plateau, the rich equestrian knowledge and stock management expertise held by the enslaved Africans, mostly from the Senegambia region in West Africa, was combined with the knowledge Indigenous workers possessed of the landscape and led to the creation of new, innovative approaches, skills, and equipment that would come to define the cowboy and his work.

One of the first innovations was using *la reata*, also known as *el lazo*, or the lasso, while on horseback. Roping had been practiced in Spain and West Africa but only on foot and generally only to rescue lone animals or to control angry bulls.[7] The more common way that the Spanish controlled cattle was through the use of the *desjarretadera*, or hocking knife. This tool, attached to a long pole, was used to sever the tendons of a bovine, thereby disabling the animal. This technique was effective but required that the animal be slaughtered where it was killed. In the early 1570s, the semi-wild cattle

Fig. 4, opposite: Heels were adopted into Western fashion at the turn of the 17th century and were first used on riding boots. English, turn of the 18th century.

Fig. 5: *Coleo a pie en Baja California Sur* (Bull-Tailing on Foot). Jesuit priest Ignacio Tirsch, 1762.

in Mexico had propagated to the point that their meat was no longer profitable, although their hides and tallow remained marketable. Opportunistic vaqueros began to hamstring and skin cattle, leaving the corpses as carrion, a practice that would be repeated centuries later on the Great Plains with the slaughter of the bison. As this indiscriminate killing increased, the use of the *desjarretadera* was banned, first for "native, mulatto, black, or mestizo" vaqueros, and then for all vaqueros.[8] The lasso then became the principal tool by which vaqueros could control cattle, and their lassoing skills from horseback became increasingly refined. The saddle was also modified through the addition of a horn for tying off the lasso and further improving its effectiveness.[9] The skills perfected by these vaqueros would become so impressive that they would eventually form a central part of rodeo entertainment in later centuries.

What the vaquero wore would also go on to inform American cowboy clothing; however, establishing how the early vaqueros dressed is difficult to determine with any certainty. Heeled riding footwear first appeared in Europe only in the seventeenth century and was initially limited to the wealthy—meaning that vaqueros would not have had access to heeled boots (fig. 4). Even eighteenth-century evidence is scant (fig. 5). By the nineteenth century, however, a clearer picture begins to emerge (fig. 6). In art, vaqueros are often depicted wearing wide-brimmed hats woven from local vegetable fiber, cotton shirts, breeches made of leather, and leather gaiters called *botas* that were wrapped around their lower legs.[10] Though adapted to local needs, nearly all of these garments had roots in Spanish or broader European traditions. Straw hats with wide brims, for example, had long been worn by European laborers. Breeches were also European, and wearing leather gaiters for riding was common in Spain. One notable distinction was footwear. Vaqueros often paired their *botas* with huaraches, traditional leather sandals dating back to precontact times. These were always worn with spurs. For added protection, vaqueros often draped animal hides suspended from the saddle across their laps and legs. These would eventually be transformed into chaps. Some nineteenth-century vaqueros added short bolero jackets and sashes to their outfits, reflecting links to the larger nineteenth-century Mexican charro fashion,[11] itself an expression of landowner status ultimately linked to the dress of Spanish bullfighters. Vaqueros also took to wearing long pants that fully buttoned up the sides as well as boots and spurs. On the range, almost all vaqueros wore serapes. These large textiles served multiple purposes—from outerwear to sleeping blankets—and represented a

Fig. 6: Vaqueros wearing *botas* in *Californians Lassoing a Steer*. August Ferran, 1849.

continuation of precontact Indigenous textile traditions, albeit in wool rather than in cotton (fig. 7).

EAST COAST COWBOYS

In the seventeenth and eighteenth centuries, as vaqueros were shaping the foundations of cowboy culture in Northern Mexico, a parallel story was unfolding in the British colonies. There the work of enslaved Africans was also central to cattle management. Most cattle in the American colonies were raised and consumed locally but, in the Carolinas, larger herds were being raised to provide hides and meat for consumption in the northern colonies or on plantations in Barbados, Jamaica, and other places in the British West Indies.

As in Spanish-controlled Mexico, the herds in the Carolinas were also open range and required rounding up, a job given specifically to enslaved Black men, mostly from Senegambia. A record from 1708 notes that, of the eighteen hundred enslaved adult men in South Carolina, a thousand were listed as "cattle hunters."[12] Although tobacco, rice, and indigo plantations competed for land, cotton cultivation had not yet taken hold, leaving space for cattle to forage. However, by the end of the eighteenth century, the invention of the cotton gin in 1793 drastically increased the profitability of cotton, pushing cattle farther west and south, eventually into Spanish-controlled Texas.

As with the early vaquero, what enslaved cow hunters wore in the eighteenth century is difficult to establish. The Negro Act of 1735 dictated that enslaved people were allowed to wear only low-quality cloth and mentions that shoes were to be supplied by enslavers. Much later accounts from formerly enslaved people make clear that many were never given footwear of any kind, regardless of the labor they performed.[13]

SHAPING THE AMERICAN MAN

As cattle economies expanded across the Americas, ideas of manliness also began to shift. Enlightenment thinking promoted concepts such as "all men are created equal," which required a redefinition of masculinity—one with the potential to enfranchise all men rather than just those of privileged birth. The new ideal was the "self-made man" who valued action over refinement—a concept that would eventually become central to

Fig. 7: *A Mexican Vaquero*.
Frederic Remington, 1890.

Fig. 8: The top boot—a knee-high black riding boot with a folded-over top in a contrasting color—was designed in the 18th century for hunting on horseback but was also worn as an item of upper-class fashion. This style of riding boot is an antecedent to the cowboy boot. English or American, early 19th century.

the creation of American identity and the valorization of the cowboy.

As the eighteenth century wore on, boots became central to this evolving ideal. In England and its colonies, the landed gentry began sporting top boots that evoked the work of running one's estates (fig. 8). Boots were also paramount to the march of imperialism and the revolutions that emerged at the end of the century. Hessian boots originated in the Austro-Hungarian Empire and featured a heart-shaped line at the top of a boot often embellished with tassels and embroidery (fig. 9). These gleaming leather boots were worn extremely small and tight fitting, often with white knit pantaloons tucked into their tops (fig. 10). Sometimes pantaloons were worn over the boot with the strap slipped under the sole and held in place by the heel. The practice of men wearing heels, however, was contentious, and Hessians began to lose favor, replaced by the Wellington boot. Named after one of Britain's most celebrated heroes—Arthur Wellesley, 1st Duke of Wellington—these boots did not hug the leg as closely. They also lacked tassels and other decorations, making them perfect for wearing under the new long-legged trousers that were replacing pantaloons.

By the middle of the nineteenth century, boots were a defining feature of manliness. In 1855, novelist Charles Dickens wrote, "There may be other integuments equally indicative of manhood, but there are none of which a male wearer is so proud of as his boots."[14] Despite this pride, very few examples of historic men's footwear have survived. The new manliness was also expressed through the rejection of fashion and sentimentality, and the majority of men did not keep things they wore. However, there are many examples of boots worn by small boys kept as keepsakes related to their "breeching." In the United States, well-to-do boys typically wore dresses until the age of five or six as part of a long tradition in Western fashion of seeking to protect boys from bad luck by dressing them as "less-desirable" girls. Breeching marked the moment when boys set aside their dresses and began wearing breeches and often boots to signify their transition from child to youth. The boots were tiny replicas of adult footwear and provide insight into the range of styles available at mid-century.[15] Unsurprisingly, the majority of these boots are Wellingtons (fig. 11).

WAR

In the first half of the nineteenth century, boots not only helped redefine manliness but were also essential to the numerous military clashes across North America (fig. 12). Spain and France contested vast territories from Louisiana to California. Mexico's War for Independence (1810–21) and the US-British War of 1812 were also part of this chaotic period, as was the simmering dispute over who "owned" Oregon Country—the Russians, Spanish, British, or Americans—which was not settled until 1846. However, the most significant conflict for the history of the cowboy and his boots was the US incursion into the Mexican state of Coahuila y Tejas. This led to the Texas Revolution in 1836 and, later, to the larger Mexican-American War (1846–48), triggered by the US annexation of Texas. The conflict ended with the United States seizing over 500,000 square miles of Mexican territory, including California, accelerating US expansion and fueling the concept of Manifest Destiny. The war also upended the delicate political balance between slave and non-slave states, setting the stage for the secession crisis that began in 1860, when South Carolina broke from the Union following Abraham Lincoln's election on an antislavery platform.[16] In all, eleven states would form the Confederate States of America, sparking the Civil War in 1861.

The tensions between North and South were complex and deeply rooted in the economic structure of each region.[17] The South had long focused on agriculture—its wealth came from cash crops cultivated for export using enslaved labor. The North, in contrast, was the center of manufacturing, including shoemaking, putting it at an advantage that not only influenced the outcome of the Civil War but also shaped the development of the cowboy boot later in the century.

Historically, footwear was essential to success in war, and the South's lack of domestic footwear-making capabilities proved to be a significant disadvantage during the Civil War.[18] Imports helped, but throughout the conflict, the South never had enough shoes, shoemaking supplies, or shoemakers. The problem was so widely understood that when Confederate General Henry Heth blamed the start of the disastrous battle at Gettysburg on the fact that his men had unknowingly "stumbled into the fight" because they were focused on "searching the town for army supplies (especially shoes)," he was believed (fig. 13).[19] Even

Fig. 9: *John Henry Manners, 5th Duke of Rutland*.
John Hoppner, 1794–96.

Fig. 10: Hessians originated in the Austro-Hungarian Empire and became fashionable in Europe and North America at the end of the 18th century. They featured curvilinear toplines and were often ornamented with embroidery and silk tassels—details that would go on to influence the development of the cowboy boot. This American version dates to the Civil War, 1861–1865.

Fig. 11: The loose-fitting and versatile Wellington boot, named after British military hero Arthur Wellesley, 1st Duke of Wellington, gained popularity in the 19th century. While few adult examples survive, child-sized versions were kept in remembrance of "breeching," when boys exchanged dresses for breeches and boots. American, 1845–1865.

after the war, the North continued to hold the advantage. Machinery—such as the Goodyear welting machine, invented in 1869—significantly improved the quality and durability of mass-produced footwear, including the cowboy boot.

BEEF BONANZA

The Civil War dramatically reshaped the American economy. The South, devastated by the conflict, struggled to recover, but the state of Texas experienced a bounty. Cattle herds left to roam during the war had exploded in size—it is estimated that there were roughly five million Texas longhorns in the state in 1865—and their unclear ownership sparked a free-for-all as many raced to claim them. The North continued to accelerate its industrialization, and its urban population surged. The market for cattle was not in the war-torn South but rather in the East, where both the expanding population and growing taste for beef increased the value of cattle. But how to get these cattle to market? The expansion of the railroads across the Great Plains provided part of the answer. If cattle could reach the railheads, they could then be transported to Upper Midwest cities—most importantly, Chicago—for slaughter and canning, which could then be shipped to the East. Driving the cattle from Texas to the more northern railheads was the other part of the equation. Herds of up to ten thousand head were driven along trails to railheads like Abilene, Kansas; Dodge City, Kansas; and Cheyenne, Wyoming. The most famous of these trails was the Chisholm Trail, which eventually stretched over eight hundred miles. Trails like this were central to transforming cattle rearing from a regional pursuit into a national enterprise. The beef bonanza had begun. (fig. 14).[20]

This expansion of the cattle economy did not, however, occur in an empty or unclaimed landscape; it ran roughshod across Indigenous lands and was facilitated by the near-total annihilation of the bison, an animal central—materially, culturally, and spiritually—to numerous Great Plains Nations. The wholesale slaughter of bison began in earnest in the 1870s, driven by both economic demand and deliberate military strategy, enabling the United States to more easily seize Indigenous lands, force Nations onto reservations, and make them dependent on the government for sustenance, including access to meat. Bison were also annihilated to clear the way for the railroads. Some were also killed for sport, their carcasses left to rot on the plains. By the end of the century, bison numbers had been reduced from an estimated sixty million to less than a thousand individual

Fig. 12: *Map of the United States of North America with Parts of the Adjacent Countries*. David H. Burr and John Arrowsmith, 1839.

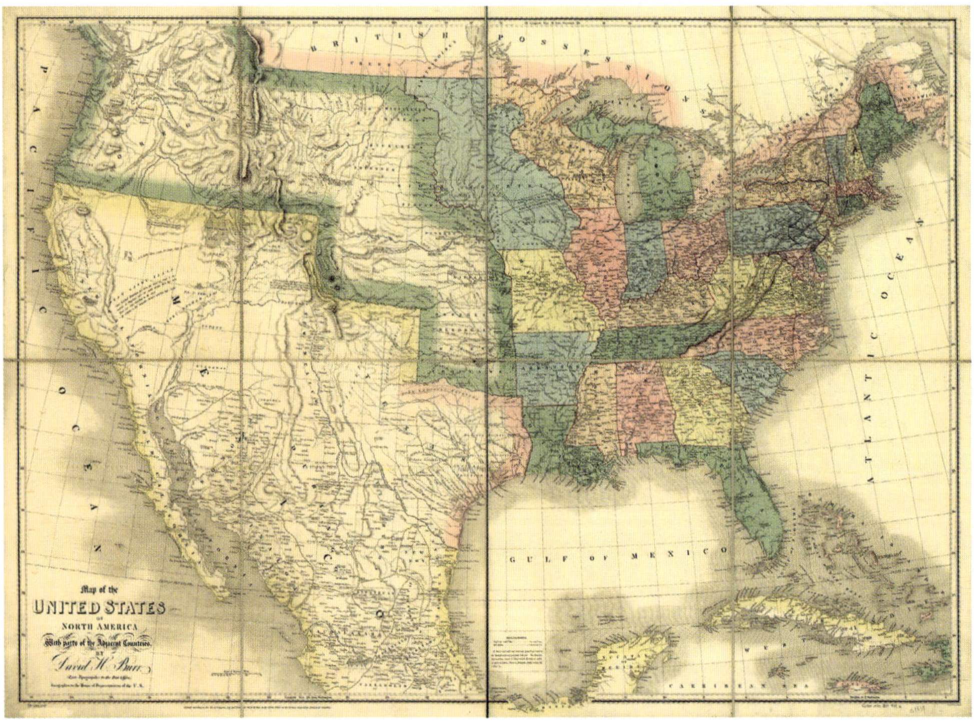

Fig. 13: *Gettysburg, Pa. Three Confederate Prisoners.* Photograph by Matthew Brady, 1863.

Fig. 14: Advertisement for St. Louis Beef Canning Co., New York City, c. 1880.

animals across both the United States and Canada. Indigenous lands were opened to cattle and settlers, and the cultural and ecological landscape of the American West profoundly changed.

THE AMERICAN COWBOY

The long cattle drives were managed by trail bosses entrusted by ranchers to get their cattle north. A typical herd of two to three thousand animals would be accompanied by a team of ten to fourteen cowboys as well as a cook, a wagon, and a wrangler for the horses.[21] It should also be noted that oftentimes these cowboys were actually boys—many began their careers in their early teens. One of the West's most famous cowboys, Nat Love, recorded in his 1907 memoir, *The Life and Adventures of Nat Love*, that he became a cowboy at the age of fifteen, only a few years after being freed from slavery. Similarly, cowboy E. C. Teddy Blue Abbott wrote in his 1939 memoir, *We Pointed Them North: Recollections of a Cowpuncher*, that he participated in his first cattle drive at the age of ten.[22] Period photographs support the youthfulness of some of these cowboys (fig. 15).

Photos also confirm the diversity of cowboys in the American West. US cattle owners employed Black, White, and Indigenous cowboys, as well as vaqueros who themselves were from long-established Indigenous, mestizo, criollo, and Black communities in Mexico. After the Civil War many formerly enslaved young men sought work away from the South, and with the increasing dispossession of Indigenous land, many Indigenous men also looked for employment. It is estimated that 20 to 25 percent of American cowboys were Black and another 10 to 15 percent were Indigenous, figures that highlight the often overlooked multicultural roots of this iconic American figure.

COWBOY CLOTHING

As low-paid, hired laborers, cowboys owned little. Yet what they did have was essential to their survival. Despite their later romanticization, most elements of cowboy attire, no matter how picturesque (figs. 16, 17, and 18), were practical. Nearly every piece of a cowboy's clothing served a specific purpose, often influenced by the long-standing workwear of the vaqueros, who had been cowboys for hundreds of years. Cowboys almost invariably wore wide-brimmed felt hats, which, like the sombrero, kept the sun off their faces and offered some protection in inclement weather (fig. 19). Cowboys also wore bandannas or silk scarves called "wild rags," which they used in a wide range of ways, including as masks to keep the dust kicked up by the cattle off of their faces and out of their lungs (fig. 15 and 16). In warm areas, cotton shirts were often worn with vests (fig. 18). While in the colder North, many added Indigenous-made buckskin clothing such as shirts that often featured beautiful embellishments including floral silk embroidery and

Fig. 15: Indigenous and Black cowboys in a photograph from the second half of the 19th century.

fringe for additional warmth (see p. 53). Many cowboys wore cowboy cuffs—wide leather "bracelets" that protected their forearms (fig. 20)—or long leather gauntlets. Some also wore chaps (sometimes called "chinks"), from the Spanish word *chaparreras* or *chaparajos,* made of cow, buffalo, or goatskin, to protect their legs (fig. 16). There were also other regional differences. In the Northern Great Plains, for example, buckaroos, an Anglicization of the term *vaquero,* wore large gauntlets and often a kind of lace-up boot called a packer boot (fig. 21). Regardless of their origins, nearly all cowboys wore spurs for communicating with their mounts (figs. 16, 17, 18, and 22).

Fig. 16: Cowboy wearing woolly chaps demonstrates twirling a lasso. Photograph published by Underwood & Underwood, c. 1891.

Fig. 17: Young cowboy in early cowboy boots, c. 1890s.

Fig. 18, opposite: Cowboys of the XIT Ranch, Texas, c. 1890.

COWBOY BOOTS

The earliest boots worn by these cowboys bore little resemblance to the modern cowboy boot. There were no pointy toes, no underslung heels or colorful inlays. Instead, early American cowboys wore whatever boots they could get (fig. 23). These were typically boots left over from wars or boots acquired from the East Coast, where shoe factories as well as smaller producers were making boots as fast as possible to send West. When the *Arabia* steamboat sank in the Missouri River on September 5,

Fig. 19: Dating all the way back to the earliest years of the vaqueros, cowboys have worn wide-brimmed hats to protect them from the elements. The most famous brand of cowboy hats, Stetson, got its start in 1865. Made of moldable felt, wearers could shape Stetsons to their liking. This style, favored by cowboy movie star Tom Mix, became an icon of Western fashion. Stetson, Tom Mix, American, 1990s.

Fig. 20: As a cowboy's boots protected the wearer's legs, cowboy cuffs were worn to protect his forearms. Like cowboy boots, they were also a site for decoration. This early 20th century pair features the very American symbolism of an eagle with a shield done in tooled leather. The tradition of tooling leather came from Spain, which itself was deeply influenced by Islamic leather artistry. American, early 20th century.

Fig. 21: Packer boots, like the more iconic pull-on cowboy boots, originated on the frontier and were also worn for horseback riding. They evolved from 19th century lace-up boots and allowed wearers to customize the fit. Like other cowboy boots, they also feature high heels and are commonly embellished with embroidery. American, Tony Lama Boots, 20th century.

Fig. 22: Spurs, like stirrups and heels, date back thousands of years. They were designed to control horses by allowing riders to prod their animals using the round metal rowels of the spurs. While all cowboys wore them, their style varied according to personal taste and region. This California-style pair features shanks decorated in silver, a 14-point starburst rowel, and metal janglers. The spur straps are decorated with tooled leatherwork with silver buckles. The maker stamp is Garza. Probably American, early 20th century.

Fig. 23: After the American Civil War, there was money to be made driving cattle from Texas up to the railways in Kansas. From there the cattle would be shipped to meat packers in Chicago and then sold as canned beef to feed the workers in factories on the East Coast. The first cowboys to do these long drives wore whatever boots they could find. This pair of boots is one example of the type early cowboys might have worn. Swiss, mid-19th century.

Fig. 24: Being a cowboy was hard on both workers and what they wore. Boots were a necessity, but demand outstripped local supply, creating opportunity for boot makers back East. This pair, made by New York City maker Gustave Jenny, is precisely the kind made for export to the West. American, 1870s–1880s.

1856, it was carrying hundreds of pairs of ready-made men's and boy's boots for the Western market by a range of East Coast makers. A pair of boots made by New York City maker Gustave Jenny is precisely the kind made for export to the West (fig. 24). Because cowboying was rough—hard on both the worker and what he wore—there was an opportunity for makers back East, but more importantly, there were opportunities for more local boot makers. These makers, in the thick of it as it were, could respond to the needs of cowboys and in doing so refine the footwear needed into what we now know as cowboy boots.

Many claimed to have invented the cowboy boot, but in reality, it was a slow process of shifts and changes. Some of the earliest modifications included the addition of a higher heel, exploiting its original function as an equestrian tool used to secure the foot in the stirrup. Vaqueros had long privileged flat-box stirrups with toe-covering tapaderos that shielded the foot and worked well with their flat-soled sandals or boots.[23] The American cowboy's preference, however, was for the ox-bow stirrup. Its rounded shape and close fit allowed the rider to rest the arch of his foot on the stirrup while his heels gave him added stability by securing the foot in the stirrup (see fig. 25).[24] In an era acutely sensitive to the idea of men in heels, the reasons for cowboys' heels were positioned as tools of the trade rather than frivolous fashion.

> For foot gear they [cowboys] invariably wear high boots, with very high heels . . . [that] are for a special purpose: or, to put it in the current scientific jargon, this highly specialized form of the heel has been developed by the requirements of the animal for some mechanical means to prevent the slipping of the foot through the aperture of the stirrup.[25]

Some, however, did make snide comments about cowboys' heels. In 1886, George W. Wingate, soldier, lawyer, and cofounder of the National Rifle Association, wrote about cowboys that:

> Some of them are as much the slaves of fashion as anyone. . . . Boots with high French heels are very popular. Our men all wore them . . . I asked them why they wore such French affairs, I was told that there was no sale in Montana for boots with anything but French heels.

Wingate's use of the term "French heels" was particularly pointed, as it was commonly associated with women's footwear at the time he was writing—especially in critiques of female vanity. Other writers also commented on cowboys wearing extremely small, tight boots that seemed to veer into Cinderella territory.

In his volume on cowboys for the series *America of the Americans: Or Builders of the Nation*, Emerson Hough wrote that cowboy boots

> [O]f fine leather, with light, narrow soles, extremely small and high heels, and fitting so tightly as to bind the foot and cramp the toes in a most vice-like grasp, surely a more irrational foot covering never was invented. Yet the cowboy wears this sort of boot, and has for a generation. His idea of "style" obliges him to cling to these peculiar boots . . . the tight, peaked, wretched cowboy boots have a great significance of their own, and may indeed be called an insignia of a calling. There is no prouder soul on earth than a cowboy.[26]

The cost of cowboy boots was another media topic and likewise raised suspicion. Their relatively high price was clearly a source of surprise as seen in this 1893 quotation from a cowboy.

> How do I dress when I'm with an outfit? Well, mostly in rags. Truth is, I do not care how I dress so long as I've got a good hat and boots and saddle . . . You can't walk in a cowboy's shoes; they fit too much. You see, we wear high-heeled boots, and get 'em as small as we can . . . Cowboys are very particular about the look of their feet and have a right to be, because they pay $15 for a pair of boots.[27]

Despite these observations, cowboys largely managed to evade criticism of their masculinity. Their swagger was seen as earned—a natural extension of their hard-living, dangerous work.

Other modifications that transitioned riding boots into cowboy boots included the use of machine stitching on the boot shaft. Stitching the boot leather to the boot lining increased the rigidity of the boot top, ensuring that it did not wrinkle and pool around the ankles, and this also provided the opportunity for decoration (fig. 25). Cowboy boots were, as Hough put it, not to be found "in the length and breadth of most large Eastern cities." Instead, these boots were specifically made for the cowboy trade. By the end

Fig. 25: As cowboy boots developed, many makers began to add machine stitching to the boot tops. Stitching the boot leather to the boot lining ensured that the shaft did not wrinkle and pool around the ankles—it also provided the opportunity for decoration. This pair features an exuberant curvilinear pattern. American, 1890s.

Fig. 26: Cowboy herding cattle in the railroad stockyards at Kansas City, Missouri, 1890s.

of the nineteenth century, the cowboy boot was well on its way to becoming an icon of the West.

THE WILD WEST

The earliest boot makers who catered specifically to the "cowboy trade" set up shop in the towns that sprang up along the route or at the terminus of the great cattle trails that emerged after the war (fig. 26). Abilene in Kansas is the quintessential example: Established in 1858 before the railway was put in, it became a bustling town when entrepreneur Joseph McCoy convinced the small railway company Hannibal and St. Joseph Railroad to ship cattle to Chicago from the depot he would build in Abilene in 1867.[28] Between 1867 and 1881 McCoy would send more than two million cattle from Abilene to Chicago.[29]

Suddenly, Abilene became the terminus of the Chisholm Trail, and almost immediately establishments such as Thomas C. McInerney's boot shop, established in 1868, opened up to meet the needs of cowboys.[30] By 1870, over 120 boot makers in Kansas were making bespoke footwear, suggesting that cowboys did in fact purchase boots after delivering their herds to the railheads.[31] Cowboys were paid only after the cattle had been delivered, and those who could afford it were eager for the baths, soft beds, new clothes, and entertainment available in these new towns (fig. 27).

Gambling, drinking, and visiting brothels were all standard in terminus towns (figs. 27 and 28). One writer quipped, "Such of the 'cowboys' as are not professional thieves, murderers and miscellaneous blacklegs . . . are men who, totally disregarding all the amenities of Eastern civilization, brook no restraint and . . . yield allegiance to no law save their own untamed passion."[32] Shoot-outs between these transient cowboys also took place, although they were less common than later storytelling would suggest. For instance, the famous military fighter and lawman Wild Bill Hickok was the marshal of Abilene and, according to him, killed *only* two people during his short tenure attempting to bring law and order to the town.[33] Stories of the "freedoms" enjoyed by cowboys, however, thrilled people back East. This was somewhat ironic given that all of these vices, including shoot-outs, were happening on the East Coast as well. The New York City shop of boot maker Gustave Jenny was the site of just such an event in 1886. Jenny had fired his journeyman, August Erkman, who later returned to the shop yelling, "You dog, you must die!" before shooting his replacement dead and then taking his own life, making *The New York Times*. For some reason, violence like this

Fig. 27: *Cowboys in a Saloon*. Charles Marion Russell, 1907.

did not lend itself to the same kind of mythmaking. Cities had cachet but were deemed dens of iniquity; the "Wild West," in contrast, was a place where men had the freedom to live exactly as they wished.

Teddy Roosevelt would become the poster boy for this idea. He was a professed overeducated Easterner who had learned to "toughen up" by spending time in the West and believed that the cowboy, while being possessed of "few of the emasculated, milk-and-water moralities admired by the pseudo-philanthropists; [he did] possess, to a very high degree, the stern, manly qualities that are invaluable to a nation."[34]

Just as these stories and ideals were emerging, the time of the trail-drive cowboy was coming to an end. Newly invented barbed wire sectioned off the open range as settlers demarcated land and sought to keep cattle out to protect crops as well as livestock from the tick-infested Texas longhorns. It was also illegal for cattle to roam across reservation lands, a restriction that cowboys often disrespected. Indeed, the phrase "cowboys and Indians," came into frequent use in the 1880s in relation specifically to conflicts caused by cattle repeatedly trespassing onto Indigenous land.[35] However, not all conflicts involved cowboys. US cavalry units, stationed in forts across the West, were the principal antagonists in the violence against Indigenous nations. These soldiers rode horses and wore boots, albeit military rather than cowboy, but they were not cowboys. Hollywood and popular fiction, however, would blur these distinctions, shaping ideas about the cowboy for generations to come.

FIRST COWBOY BOOT MAKERS

Many of the most famous cowboy boot manufacturers trace their history back to this period of long-distance cattle drives. Mythology holds that there were only three boot makers—Cubine, Hyer, and Justin—making cowboy boots in the early years, but as historian Barbara Brackman has proved, hundreds of boot makers worked across the West—1,274 were counted in the *Tenth Census: Report on the Manufactures of the United States West of the Iowa Louisiana Line* as working in 1880.[36] Nevertheless, it is indisputable that each of these three names would be important to the history of cowboy boots.

John W. Cubine, originally from Virginia, was a shoemaker by trade and set up shop in Coffeyville, Kansas, after fighting for the Confederate Army.[37] He is said to have created boots modeled on military footwear and is credited with being the first to offer boots in lefts and rights, a trend that had started much earlier in the century. Charles Albert Hyer, the son of a shoemaker, opened Hyer Boots in Olathe, Kansas, in late 1880.[38] Exactly when Herman Joseph Justin arrived in Texas is difficult to ascertain, but Brackman dates his arrival to the early to mid-1880s. He seems to have first worked at the Norton Shoe Shop in Gainesville.[39] He then moved to the Chisholm Trail town of Spanish Fort, Texas, but after the town went bust in 1887, Justin married Annie Allen, and by 1889 the couple had moved to Nocona, Texas, where Justin became the town's largest employer.[40] Both companies offered custom boots for clients in the area, but they also increased their reach by leveraging the ever-expanding railways and postal system to accept custom orders and deliver finished boots. Industrialization had brought about the mass production of shoes and the standardization of shoe sizing. Hyer and Justin relied on some machinery to make their boots, but their mail-order measurement kits still offered significant customization. The forms instructed customers on how to measure their feet. Later order forms also asked customers to specify toe and heel shape as well as heel height. This service allowed boot makers to spread their boots and reputations far and wide.

Lucchese was also founded at the end of the nineteenth century. Its founder, Salvatore Lucchese, emigrated with his brother Joseph from Palermo, Italy, to Galveston, Texas, in 1882. Sons of a shoemaker, they opened a boot making shop near Fort Sam Houston in San Antonio, Texas, the following year. One of Salvatore's interests was new shoemaking machinery, which he enthusiastically embraced. In fact, each of these early boot makers—Hyer, Justin, and Lucchese—set the stage for what would eventually become the modern cowboy boot, blending traditional craftsmanship with emerging industrial techniques and expanding their reach far beyond the frontier through railroads and mail-order catalogues. However, as the railways were transporting their boots to customers, the days of the actual cowboy were numbered. These same networks of transportation made long-distance trail drives increasingly unnecessary. The open range was now crisscrossed with barbed wire, towns and villages claimed more and more land, and cattle were increasingly contained on ranches, transforming the cowboy into a ranch hand. What the cowboy symbolized, however, was only just beginning to take shape.

Fig. 28: *Saloon Girl with Drunken Cowboy*. Charles Marion Russell, c. 1898.

Fig. 1: Smoked deer hide "fireman's shirt" and leggings with Norway House–style embroidery, made by a Cree-Métis ancestor, 1870–90.

Fig. 2: Studio portrait of a man wearing a fringed buckskin jacket, fringed chaps, and embroidered gauntlets. His lace-up leather shoes give away that he is not an actual cowboy. Late 19th century.

FRINGE, FLORALS, AND BUCKSKIN: INDIGENOUS AESTHETIC INFLUENCE IN PLAINS COWBOY FASHION

Justine Woods

Enduring images of the cowboy in the Great Plains nod to a stylistic evolution of cowboy fashion that emerged at the seams of deep intercultural exchange. By the nineteenth century, prior nomadic ways of life in the Great Plains adjusted to a new social system defined by pastoralism and the fur trade prompted by an influx of European traders, allowing for new interactive zones to emerge.[1] It is within these interactive zones where Indigenous design theory and methods and European aesthetics begin to merge, impacting and evolving the style, function, and material meaning of cowboy dress to come.

Cowboy dress in the Great Plains depended on functional garments, including high-heeled boots, spurs, and chaps, also known in the northern plains as "woolies."[2] Originally developed in California, chaps made their way into plains cowboy attire by way of

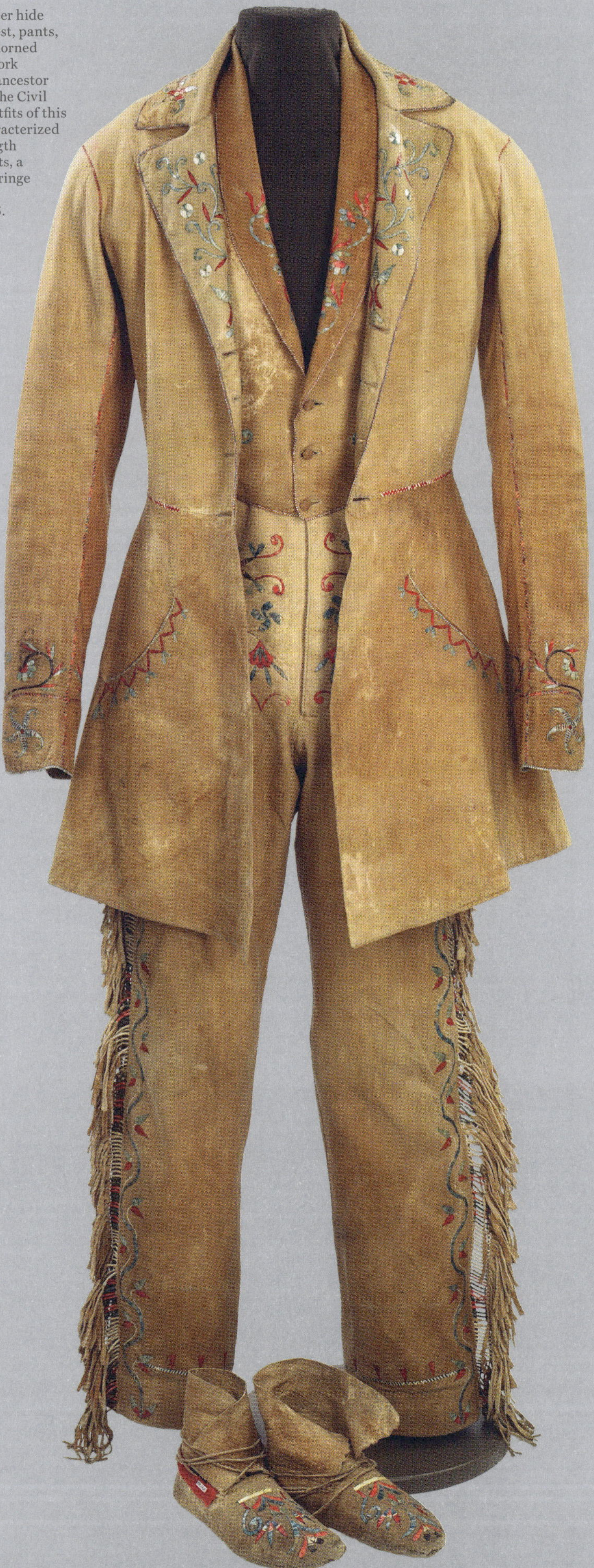

Fig. 3: Smoked deer hide tailored jacket, vest, pants, and moccasins adorned with floral quillwork made by a Métis ancestor designer. Before the Civil War, buckskin outfits of this fashion were characterized by their knee-length skirts, fitted waists, a lapel collar, and fringe welted into the seams. 1845–1865.

Fig. 4: Portrait of American army scout, buffalo hunter, and showman William "Buffalo Bill" Cody wearing a beaded buckskin jacket, beaded gauntlets, and over-the-knee leather boots. Late 19th century.

vaqueros who drove cattle from Oregon to Montana in the 1860s.[3] The stylistic origin of chaps is rooted in Indigenous fashion history, particularly evolving from Indigenous leggings (figs. 1 and 3). Leggings and crotchless pants exemplify ancient fashion design practice and are some of the first examples of Indigenous dress alongside moccasins, existing before the adoption of breechcloths and shirts.[4] Leggings were made in response to a deep consideration and reciprocal awareness of land, providing warmth and protection from surrounding brush. After breechcloths evolved into pants, leggings were still worn on top in the winter season for additional warmth and protection from harsh winds.[5] Honoring preceding design knowledge, chaps became a staple garment in plains cowboy dress, serving to protect the body from abrasive environmental elements.[6] Fringe was a common embellishment found on chaps in the northern plains and later evolved as a universal identifier of cowboy fashion propagated through popular culture and mass media. Fringe as a trim, edging, and adornment technique can be traced back to early Egyptian and Mesopotamian weaving and textile methods.[7] Within Indigenous fashion contexts across Turtle Island, fringe is used for its stylistic vibrance and functional properties by multiple Indigenous nations in tandem with their own individual material aesthetics. Made by cutting thin strips of animal hide, fringe reflects and wicks moisture from rain or snow, preventing water from seeping through the garment and allowing the body to remain dry in wet and cold conditions.[8]

With the introduction of European trade goods such as steel needles, glass seed beads, and woolen cloth, Indigenous designers actively responded to shifts in material access, adapting their designs accordingly. Imported cloth and clothing began to co-exist with Indigenous design methods, resulting in a hybrid use of aesthetics, techniques, and materials.[9] Particularly in the northern plains, a demand for an aesthetic that was elegant yet still "frontiersy" resulted in a European tailored suit jacket and pants made from buckskin, adorned with floral beadwork or quillwork (fig. 2).[10] Innovatively designed and constructed by First Nations and Métis women, the ensemble proved to be well suited for those working as fur traders, mountain men, or frontier scouts.[11] At the same time, the adoption of buckskin tailored jackets became a popular choice of dress for showmen and dramatists such as William "Buffalo Bill" Cody (see fig. 3). Beginning in the 1880's, Cody's "Wild West Show" romanticized settler-colonial dominance over Indigenous lands and resources, replacing Indigenous narratives of land with colonial narratives of conquest.[12] Posing in black-and-white portraits wearing a buckskin beaded jacket, Cody's aesthetic portrayal underlines an ideological and ecological imperialism that severs the Indigenous body from its deep kinship with land, animals, and ultimately itself (fig. 4).[13] The buckskin jacket is therefore stripped of its spiritual intentions, purpose, and meaning, and regurgitated as a glorified symbol of the "wild" west.

RODEO

As the nineteenth century drew to a close, so too did the era of the open-range cowboy. Yet rather than fading into history, the cowboy's cultural significance only intensified. Though he was a product of the modern age—his existence tied to railroads and the rise of the industrial meat complex—he was about to be transformed into a symbol of a bygone golden age in America. His cowboy boots, once purely utilitarian, would likewise be reimagined as bold, iconic statements, embellished and stylized to suit the new myth in the making.

NATION BUILDING

Driven by the desire to craft a distinctly American national identity, the reinvention of the cowboy began at the turn of the twentieth century. Between 1880 and 1920, immigration surged, sparking anxieties about national cohesion and what it meant to be American. The West, both real and imagined, was seen as the crucible in which immigrants, specifically those from Europe, could be transformed into "true" Americans.[41] The cowboy, once a multiethnic laborer, was recast as White and, in this new guise, embodied the ideal of the self-made man whose rugged individualism had enabled him to pull himself up by his bootstraps. As this idealized version of American manliness took shape, the image of the cowboy began to change. His clothing, and most notably his boots, became increasingly decorative and evolved into a kind of costume designed to amplify his swagger.

COWBOY COSTUME

The reframing of the cowboy began in the 1870s and 1880s with dime novels that told of the colorful exploits of Western characters. These stories were brought to life by Buffalo Bill Cody, who reenacted his exploits onstage in theatrical interpretations of frontier clothing and full stage makeup. By 1883, he had created his famous Wild West show, a "half-circus, half-history lesson"[42] that was instrumental in constructing the narrative about how the West was "won" (fig. 1). Buffalo Bill had started out as a cowboy at the age of eleven and went on to be a fur trapper, gold miner, pony express rider, soldier, bison hunter, and eventually combined all of these experiences into his role as showman. His shows, and the others that followed, were extremely popular in both the United States and Europe, and started to promote a visual vocabulary for cowboys. Photography studios also played a pivotal role in fixing and spreading the image of the cowboy. By the late nineteenth century, clients could pay to be dressed up in "cowboy" costume wearing chaps, hats, and holding guns. Often, however, boots were not offered, and instead these make-believe cowboys were captured wearing their own street shoes. Film shortly followed. Some of the earliest motion pictures featured cowboys, but while some aspects of cowboy attire were being codified, the boots had yet to capture attention. This, however, would begin to change by the 1910s, when boots began to be made more decorative.

FOREIGN INFLUENCE

At the end of the nineteenth century, the stitching on cowboy boot tops became increasingly decorative. The designs, often highly curvilinear, were new, but they were also somehow familiar (fig. 2). In many ways these designs were in sympathy with similar embellishments found on the Zouave uniforms that had taken fashion by storm in the middle of the century, influencing everything from women's jackets to Civil War uniforms. The original Zouave troops came from Algeria, and the most decorative elements of their outfits were their jackets, which often featured braid or cord laid out into curvilinear shapes in addition to cloth appliqué stars. Not only were they distinctive for what they wore but the Zouaves were also revered as an elite fighting force, making France one of the most respected armies in the Western world. In the middle of the century, a Zouave "craze" gripped the United States, and when the Civil War broke out, both Northern and Southern soldiers created Zouave regiments mimicking the dress of these Algerian fighters (fig. 3). The extremely wide reach of this visual language in military and civilian fashion should be considered in relation to the decoration seen on early cowboy boots, especially the penchant for curvilinear stitching on boot shafts and the frequent use of appliqué stars.

FASHION OF THE TIMES

Considering the impact of Zouave fashion on the decoration of cowboy boots is important because the boots did not evolve in cultural isolation; their development was in fact embedded in broader fashion trends. For example, the pointed toe on cowboy boots is often described as having been invented for reasons of practicality—a pointed toe allows the foot to slip more easily into and out of a stirrup. This may be true, but it does not appear to have been the original inspiration. Narrower toes did not emerge in cowboy boots until the late nineteenth century, which is when pointy-toed footwear became extremely fashionable for men in general (fig. 4). A survey of mail-order catalogues from the 1890s—such as Montgomery Ward and Sears, Roebuck—illustrates the availability of this style.

At the same time that pointy toes were in fashion, another hallmark of cowboy boots—wrinkles across the instep—was also introduced as a broader fashion trend. These intentional creases, sometimes pressed and sometimes sewn, were designed to help a worn shoe maintain a neater appearance. The popularity of this detail even led to the invention of vamp-creasing machines. Although the fashion eventually faded, vamp creasing remained a staple of shoemaking into the early twentieth century; a 1918 report from the US Bureau of Labor Statistics, *Descriptions of Occupations: Boots and Shoes, Harness and Saddlery, Tanning*, notes that young boys and girls were specifically employed in factories as vamp creasers.[43]

The distinctive embroidery often found on the toe of cowboy boots, called a "toe bug," or "toe flower," also emerged during this period. A shoe made by Hurley Shoe Company for the 1893 World's Columbian Exposition in Chicago showcases many decorative elements that would later define cowboy boot ornamentation (fig. 5).[44] Like vamp creases, the toe bug would go on to become a feature of cowboy boots specifically.

DISTINCTIVE DESIGN

Despite the links to larger fashion trends, cowboys *were* beginning to acquire a more distinctive look, but was it reflective of what cowboys were actually wearing, or was a divergence developing between what the idealized cowboy wore compared to actual working ranch hands? A newspaper article from 1909 reported that:

> The long spike-heel cowboy boots of the western plans have gone to the discard. In their place have come boots with broad military heels . . . In the days of old a boot with a three or four inch spiked heel was just as essential to the welfare and comfort of a cowpuncher as was a six-shooter . . . But times have changed and with them the

Fig. 1, previous page: Through dime novels and Wild West shows, the dress and culture of Indigenous peoples began to be ossified and othered. Famed Húŋkpapȟa Lakȟóta leader Tȟatȟáŋka Íyotake (Buffalo Bull Who Sits Down) with Buffalo Bill Cody, 1897.

Fig. 2: Before decorative stitching became a hallmark of cowboy boots, European and the East Coast boot makers began experimenting with embroidery on men's boots. This was often done on "prize work" created to demonstrate the skill of the boot maker. This pair features elements that would eventually decorate cowboy boots, including whimsical stitching and appliqué leather stars. European, 1840s.

style of cowboy boots. Most of the big western ranches have been cut-up and fenced. The cattle have been tamed. A cowboy spends almost as much time on foot around the corrals or fixing fences as he spends in the saddle. Therefore a new heel had to be adopted; one that would protect him in the saddle and make walking easy. He found the combination in the two inch military heel.[45]

This article assuredly was reporting a shift in what was actually being worn, but the idea of a cowboy in "sensible" shoes was not romantic. The tension between reality and representation was growing. Cowboy boots, once defined by terrain and labor, were increasingly being shaped by fashion and performance. As cowboy life became entertainment, the gear—especially the boots—had to keep pace with the spectacle.

ENTERTAINMENT

Although cowboys as entertainment were entering a golden age at the turn of the century, they had been thrilling crowds for decades in rodeos. Mexican vaqueros had long performed extraordinary feats of riding and roping during roundups, which eventually developed into *charreadas*—Mexican rodeos—linked to Spanish bullfighting festivals and equestrian spectacles. By the mid-nineteenth century, these roundups had evolved into ever more spectacular forms of public entertainment across the United States, with places such as Santa Fe, New Mexico; Deer Trail, Colorado; and Pecos, Texas, each claiming to have hosted the first American rodeo.[46] At the center of these performances was the display of man's control over animals, but they also spoke to nation building through the celebration of individual grit and perseverance.

The Wild West shows that emerged at the end of the nineteenth century

Fig. 3: Second Lt. Orange Fuller Dorrance of the Union Army 28th Iowa Infantry wearing a zouave-inspired jacket. Carte de visite by J.A. Sheldon of New Orleans, Louisiana.

Fig. 4: Many 20th-century cowboy boots feature very narrow toes, often explained as a practical design for slipping into stirrups. This may be the effect but not the cause. Cowboy boots did not evolve in isolation, instead their development reflected broader fashion trends. In the 1890s and into the early 20th century, pointy-toed footwear became extremely fashionable, as exemplified by this pair. Possibly French, 1890s.

Fig. 5: This "prizework" shoe made by Hurley Shoe Company for the 1893 World's Columbian Exposition in Chicago showcases many decorative elements that would later define cowboy boot ornamentation, including vamp creases and the toe bug. Collection of the Buttonwoods Museum.

borrowed rodeo elements like bronco busting but expanded their scope. They staged reenactments of famous battles between American fighters and Indigenous nations, framing Indigenous participants as "savage" antagonists, who were "worthy" opponents, but were ultimately doomed by their resistance to "civilization." The stereotypes about Indigenous people created and perpetuated by these shows was not fleeting; they lingered for generations in the popular imagination, shaping millions of spectators' ideas about Indigenous identity and history. The narrative was always clear: Indigenous resistance could be admired for its "futile" bravery but Indigenous culture was a part of the past.

Many Wild West shows also featured riders from North Africa and the Caucasus. The exploits of these expert horseman were also treated as exotic spectacles, thrilling to audiences for both their skill and otherness highlighted in great part by how they were dressed. Their presence, like that of Mexican vaqueros, Black cowboys, and trick-riding women, all of whom were highly skilled, positioned these performers as novelties (fig. 6). Indeed, the very diversity of the cast served to frame the White cowboy—and his costuming—as the embodiment of Americanness.

REEL COWBOYS

Not only were these new representations of the cowboy being promoted through novels and Wild West shows, cinema was also entering the fray at the end of the nineteenth century and the cowboy was a favorite subject. One of the first to put the cowboy on-screen was Thomas Edison, who filmed Buffalo Bill Cody and his Wild West show during a tour stop in New York City in 1894. As the medium evolved, so too did the Western genre, and the look of the Hollywood cowboy became more formulaic. "Good" cowboys were portrayed as moral, hardworking, loyal, and patriotic. They were also young and handsome—admired and desired in equal measure—and their costume served not only to enhance their physical appeal but also to signal their character.

In the earliest years of film, cowboy boots were not particularly distinctive,

but by the 1910s, they started to become more clearly a part of the costuming. Influenced by the growing theatricality of cowboy culture, cowboy boots in general started to become more decorative. In 1908, Hough wrote that some cowboy boots made for the trade now featured fancy tops in bright-colored leather, adding that boots from Texas, in particular, frequently had ornamentation.[47] Edwin Legrand Sabin in *Bar B Boys: Or, The Young Cow-Punchers* from 1909 describes a pair of cowboy boots in soft brown goatskin leather and red tops decorated with silver filigree,[48] while C. R. Rasmussen's 1912 *Dictionary of Footwear* defined cowboy boots as being made of calfskin, with tops decorated with fancy stitching and high heels with small bottoms.[49] Author Willa Cather described another tantalizing pair in her 1918 novel, *My Ántonia*, writing that they were "stitched in bold design—roses, and true-lover's knots, and undraped female figures," which the owner, farmhand Otto Fuchs, "solemnly explained, were angels."[50] Justin's and Hyer's catalogues from 1919 and 1920 also show just how much inlay, overlay, and stitching work had increased in popularity (fig. 7).

In part, this new trend was influenced by what "reel" cowboys such as Tom Mix wore on-screen and in real life (figs. 8 and 9). Blucher Boots made one of Mix's favored models that featured a design of stitched tulips and inlay diamonds along the top line. Blucher Custom Boot Company was started by C. G. "Gus" Blucher and Archer LaForce in 1915. They had both worked for the Justin Boot Company before striking out on their own and setting up shop in Cheyenne, Wyoming.[51] The partnership did not last, and LaForce went on to start the Western Boot Company while Blucher moved his operation to Olathe, Kansas.[52] Blucher Boots became renowned for its detailed custom work.

The introduction of color film in the middle of the 1920s only heightened the appeal of vibrantly decorated boots, making their bold hues even more striking on-screen. The color sequences in the 1924 silent film *The Wanderer* set the stage for flashy, eye-catching boots as an essential part of the cowboy's cinematic identity. As more filmmakers used Technicolor in the 1930s and 1940s, elaborately inlaid and brightly dyed cowboy boots became a visual shorthand for the

Fig. 6: *Buffalo Bill's Wild West and Congress of Rough Riders of the World In the Grandest of Illuminated Arenas, 2 Electric Plants, 250,000 Candle Power.* The Springer Litho. Co., 1895.

idealized cowboy, reinforcing their status as both a practical necessity and a symbol of showmanship. These decorative costumes were not without their critics; the term *drugstore cowboys* goes back at least to 1918 and was used to mock those who simply played cowboys rather than being actual cowboys.

DUDE RANCHES

Interest in highly decorative cowboy boots was driven not only by cinema; it was also driven by postwar realities. Europe had suffered devastating damage, making European holidays impossible for wealthy Americans in the immediate postwar years. Suddenly, dude ranches became very appealing, as did national parks, and both required specialized gear to be enjoyed (figs. 10 and 12). Dude ranches first developed in the late nineteenth century, when ranchers struggling to make ends meet would sometimes accept boarders. In the beginning these were often young men from the East—"dudes" or city slickers—looking to "toughen up" and try out the cowboy lifestyle. Teddy Roosevelt credited staying on a ranch in his youth for changing the entire trajectory of his life. Some ranches also hosted hunting parties. Over time, many of these ranches became luxurious vacation destinations, offering affluent Easterners the promise of rejuvenation in the "unspoiled" wilderness. The plain, practical cowboy boot served its function, but it lacked the romance vacationers craved. These guests wanted boots adorned with intricate embroidery, leather inlays, detailed tooling, and decorative appliqué—they wanted boots that looked like the ones worn by the heroes and heroines of the movies. As *Vogue* put it in 1928, dude ranching combined "the healthfulness of a cure with the amusement of being part of a gaily colored 'movie' cast."[53] The article also noted that while many of the garments worn on dude ranches "would look impossibly garish at home . . . how attractive they are in the right setting."[54] These boots, however, were not cheap, costing "anything one is extravagant enough to pay for them."[55]

RUSSIAN DRESSING

Just as in earlier periods, the cowboy boots of the 1920s were embedded in larger cultural moments and broader fashion trends. One of the most

Fig. 7: Cover of C. H. Hyer and Son's catalog, 1920.

intriguing and perhaps consequential factors creating the appetite for highly ornate cowboy boots was the explosion of interest in Russian design in this decade.

The Russian Revolution and Russia's role in World War I brought Russian folk costume into focus, and suddenly, designers and consumers alike were interested in fashions that reflected Russian aesthetics, from intricate embroidery to brightly colored leatherwork (fig. 11). Article after article encouraged American women to add Russian touches to their outfits, while retailers promoted accessories such as "Russian boots," often ornamented with inlay or overlay leatherwork. Given the

Fig. 8: Pair of boots worn by Tom Mix, c. 1920s.

popularity of these Russian-inspired styles, it should come as no surprise that the decorative leatherwork found on cowboy boots in the 1920s might share a similar visual language, especially if some of the target customers were wealthy Easterners fluent in the nuances of fashion. The larger public awareness of Russia, combined with the influx of immigrants from Russia and surrounding regions, clearly could have influenced cowboy boot makers, either consciously or not, contributing to the richness and range of their decorative vocabulary.

COWGIRLS

The majority of these highly decorative cowboy boots were worn by men, but women increasingly wanted to participate in the romance of the West as well. Some purchased cowboy boots to vacation as cowgirls on dude ranches (fig. 13). Others, however, took a more active role, entering the rodeo circuit that had replaced the Wild West shows. In the early 1920s, a growing number of women became professional rodeo performers, competing in bronc busting, relay racing, trick riding, and steer roping—carrying forward the spirit of legendary sharpshooter Calamity Jane and famed rodeo cowgirl Lucille Mulhall.

The daring performances of riders such as Prairie Rose Henderson, Mabel Strickland Woodward, and Tad Lucas briefly brought rodeo cowgirls into the spotlight. Yet as rodeo became increasingly commercialized, concerns about women risking bodily harm led many organizers to restrict or fully ban their participation. Just as the cowgirl was the exception to the rule in the Wild West shows, rodeo stars likewise remained exceptions. Cowboy boots for women were, accordingly, positioned more as decorative accessories appropriate for watching—rather than participating in—rodeos (fig. 14).

AMERICAN FOLK DRESS

The Roaring Twenties came to a screeching halt with the New York stock market crash on October 29, 1929. Not only did an economic collapse ensue, the entire world was plunged into the chaos that would eventually lead to World War II. The fragile peace established at the end of World War I haunted the 1930s, and a new, more virulent strain of nationalism emerged, driven by the "science" of eugenics and visions of racial and cultural "purity." Many countries looked backward to imaginary "better times," and suddenly, agrarian folk dress became a potent symbol of stability and tradition.

Fig. 9: Tom Mix in *Prairie Trails*, 1920.

Fig. 10: *Southwestern Dude Ranches*, advertisement for Santa Fe Railway. Hernando G. Villa, 1931.

In the United States, the constructed image of the cowboy would once again be pressed into service to help define what it meant to be American.

Despite the economic hardships of the Depression, dude ranches remained popular vacation destinations. US president Franklin Delano Roosevelt, a distant relative of Teddy Roosevelt's, saw their promotion as part of the means to stimulate local economies and keep money in the United States. The ranches, along with the cowboy, also served as reminders of what defined America identity and values as the world headed into another war. As more and more people began to don Western attire while vacationing, one humorous newspaper article from 1940 wrote that many a cowboy had abandoned "chaps and high-heeled boots and shirts with many buttons and all the rest of his once colorful gear, for oxfords, slacks and sports shirts. It seems that cowboys do not want to look like the boarders." Despite this story, the cowboy "look" mattered. The invention of the roper boot was born out of the need to meet the expectations of how cowboys should look. In the 1930s, rodeo performers, especially trick riders, began wearing sneakers (fig. 15). The Rodeo Cowboy Association committee started to fret that this very non-cowboyish footwear did not match the look the crowd expected. Finally, a few years after the war, Justin Boots created the roper boot that performers would be obliged to wear. The boot the company designed was not showy, but it was practical, and the lower leg shaft was in keeping with the fashion in cowboy boots (fig. 16).

The importance of the cowboy look to American identity was also seen in the choice of the Leathers family as winners of the Typical American Family Contest held in 1939 at the New York World's Fair.[56] The Leathers were ranchers from Texas, and a photo of the family shows the father and son displaying their low-shaft "peewee" boots with their pant legs stuffed

Fig. 11: The Russian Revolution and Russia's role in World War I sparked a fascination with Russian folk costume in the late 1910s and 1920s. Leather overlays and bold colors influenced fashion footwear such as these yellow high heels. Swedish, 1920s.

Fig. 12: After World War I, Hollywood, dude ranches, and rodeos helped to glamorize the cowboy boot. These flashy rodeo riders from 1928 wear a range of colorful boots. Cowboys and riders sit along a fence at the San Antonio Rodeo, Texas, 1928.

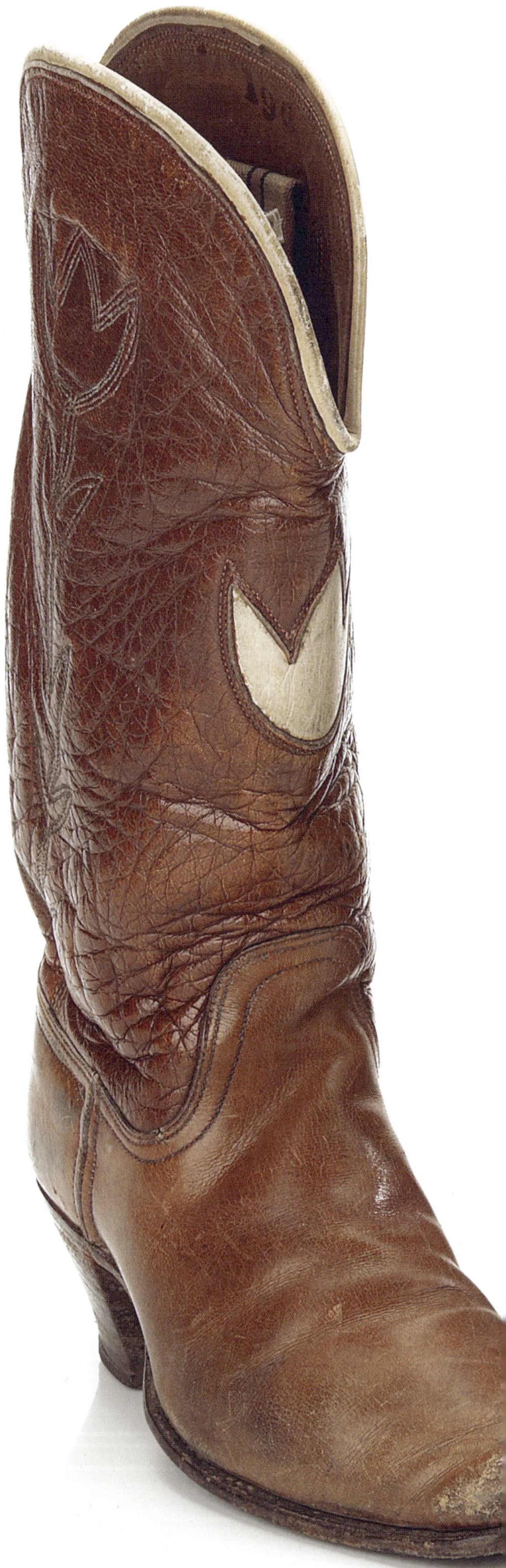

Fig. 13: These cowboy boots were worn by Margaret Brazeau (née Fry) in Calgary Stampede parades in the early 1920s. They are decorated with the popular tulip design favored by cowboy film star Tom Mix. They were made by Calgary-based Riley & McCormick Co. Ltd, which specialized in custom-made saddles, boots, and other leather goods. Riley & McCormick Co. Ltd, Canadian, 1922–1924. Collection of Glenbow Museum.

Fig. 14: A woman displays cowboy boot designs in Fort Worth in 1928.

inside. The daughter also wears cowboy boots. Few Americans were ranchers in 1939, yet the Leathers and their Western aesthetic spoke to the moment. They were White (as were all the contestants), hardworking, linked to the Western landscape, and exemplified "Americanism of name and ancestors."[57] The impression given was that the family was no-nonsense, with their decorative cowboy boots adding just the right amount of Americana.

By the 1930s, decorative cowboy boots were to be expected wherever cowboy boots were appropriate—be it at a rodeo, a dude ranch, or any American celebration—as an expression of national dress. The newest addition to cowboy boot fashion was the shorter shaft style known as peewees, popular with both men and women. Peewees tended to be highly decorated, but taller boots were decorated, too (fig. 19). Flowers and butterflies were popular motifs (figs. 17 and 18). Abstract patterns, often vaguely reminiscent of Indigenous designs, could also be found (figs. 20 and 21). The market for these boots was growing, and soon, companies offered cowboy boots for the whole family.

OLD HANDS AND NEW PLAYERS

As interest in cowboy boots grew, many heritage brands thrived. C. H. Hyer died in 1921, leaving the business to his sons—and the business continued to grow. H. J. Justin had passed away just three years earlier leaving the company in the hands of his three sons who moved the operation from Nocona to Fort Worth in 1924. The move meant easier access to railway distribution, and as the brothers industrialized their boot-making process, their production capabilities dramatically increased (fig. 23).

One Justin, however, was not happy with the move. H. J. Justin's daughter Enid Justin took umbrage at her brothers' decision and declined to relocate. Instead, in 1925 she opened her own cowboy boot company, Nocona Boots, in her father's old factory and began making beautiful boots equal in quality to those of her brothers (figs. 22 and 24). Miss Enid, as she was called, was a bit of an anomaly, as women did not make cowboy boots or own cowboy boot companies. Yet, despite what the larger public thought, women had long worked in the industry sewing boot tops. Miss Enid herself had stitched boot tops for her father. In fact, women were employed by the thousands sewing footwear uppers for manufacturers across the country,

Fig. 15: Equestrian trick rider wearing sneakers, c. 1930s.

Fig. 16: In the 1930s, rodeo performers, especially trick riders, began wearing sneakers. The Rodeo Cowboy Association committee worried that this non-cowboy footwear didn't match crowd expectations. In 1954, Justin Boots was asked to create the Roper Boot. The black boot was not showy, but it was practical, and the lower leg shaft was in keeping with the fashion of cowboy boots. Justin Boots, American, 1980s.

Fig. 17: By the 1930s, decorative cowboy boots were common. Floral and butterfly inlays were especially popular, alongside more abstract patterns. This men's pair features inlaid butterflies and flowers, created by cutting shapes into the shaft leather and filling the voids with colored leather, then securing them with decorative stitching. The saw-tooth leather collar, overlaid onto the shaft, adds further embellishment. G. C. Blucher, American, 1930s.

Fig. 18, opposite: Detail of boots on pp. 80–81.

Fig. 19: Young woman at a rodeo in Ashland, Montana, wearing inlaid butterfly boots, 1941.

yet completing a boot was considered a man's job (fig. 25).

In 1929 Salvatore Lucchese passed away and, as with other early cowboy boot makers, his son also took over the business. The Lucchese name continued to build its reputation for quality footwear, and the rich and famous increasingly flocked to the brand. Tony Lama established his boot-making business in 1911, but rose to prominence after World War II (figs. 26 and 27). Another significant maker, Acme Boots, was founded by Jessel Cohn and his son Sidney. Initially focused on children's footwear, the company relocated to Tennessee in 1935 and began manufacturing colorful cowboy boots. Aggressively marketed to men, women, and children, Acme became one of the most prolific producers of cowboy boots in the twentieth century (fig. 28).

BESPOKE BOOTS

As the mass production of cowboy boots continued to expand, a number of boot makers decided to focus on crafting bespoke boots. Arguably the most famous was Charlie Dunn. He was born into a

Fig. 20: Wearing cowboy boots to the annual Calgary Stampede is a Canadian tradition. This pair, purchased for the event in the 1950s, shows only gentle wear, suggesting they were not part of everyday attire. The intricate inlay work gives the boots an almost eyelet-like appearance. Despite decorative details such as hearts and stars, there is nothing overtly gendered about this pair. Probably Canadian, 1950. Generous gift of June Murdoch.

Fig. 21: A pair of inlaid cowboy boots with one foot in the stirrups, c. 1950.

Fig. 22: Enid Justin, 1930–1940. After her father—the founder of Justin Boots—passed away, her brothers decided to move the company to Fort Worth, Texas. Miss Enid, as she preferred, refused and instead started her own rival company, Nocona Boots.

shoemaking family in 1898 that moved to Paris, Texas, and he reportedly made his first pair of boots when he was just a child.[58] Eventually he would be hailed as the Michelangelo of cowboy boots. His detailed and precise work often included celebrated designs such as yellow leather roses, overlay cacti paired with barbed wire, and his signature writ large in fine stitches running up the sides of the boots (figs. 29, 30, and 33). However, Dunn's true artistry lay in the fit of the boots he made. In keeping with the master-apprentice shoemaking tradition, Dunn took on Lee Miller, who to this day makes boots that continue to reflect what he learned from Dunn, who passed away in 1993.

Ray Jones, another master boot maker, was born in Oklahoma in 1918 and raised in Dallas. He first learned leatherwork and saddle making before turning to boots.[59] In 1938, he and his wife set up shop in Lampasas, Texas, where he became known for building hard-wearing boots that were understated in their elegance. He brought a crispness to his work that the boots retained long after they were worn. He was known for beading (also called piping) the side seams of his boots using white leather, and he pegged his shanks using three rows of pegs.[60] He also made fancy top boots, but he preferred stitched ones. He supposedly offered his customers one of two stitching patterns, but people joked that he really only did one of the patterns as he seemed to hate the other.[61] Other hallmarks of his work include an arrow-shaped tongue and his distinctive toe bug, which features two large "leaves" that droop almost like a handlebar mustache along the sides of the toes (fig. 31). As Jones's success grew, so did his shop, and many who worked under him went on to become master boot makers themselves. Pablo Jass, working today, is considered Jones's true heir. Despite Jones's lack of variety, many of his customers considered him the best boot maker to have ever lived. Jones stopped making boots in 1983 and passed away in 1996.[62]

Willie Lusk was born in 1914 and entered the trade as a teenager, likewise becoming one of the most sought-after boot makers in Texas. He first learned the craft at N. A. Brown's in San Angelo before moving on to work with Brown's brother E. E. Brown in Lubbock, Texas. When E. E. Brown closed his shop, Lusk's

Fig. 23: Herman Joseph Justin arrived in Texas sometime in the early 1880s, working in several places before settling in Nocona to establish his company. He offered custom boots for clients in the area but also expanded his reach by leveraging the ever-expanding railways and postal system to accept custom orders and deliver finished boots. This pair was purchased in the 1940s. Justin Boots, American, 1940s. Generous gift of Col. Marvin Rich.

Fig. 24: One of the new cowboy boot companies to emerge in the 1920s was Nocona Boots, founded by Enid Justin. This is a pair of men's peewees, a new style that became fashionable in the 1930s. Nocona Boots, American, 1930s–1940s.

Fig. 25: Female business owners were extremely rare, but almost all the decorative work on cowboy boots was sewn by women. Hyer factory, c. 1940s.

exceptional craftsmanship had already earned him a devoted clientele—including infamous gambler Benny Binion, who offered to finance Lusk's own venture, Lusk's Boot Shop. Lusk's fame grew rapidly, not only because of his meticulous workmanship but also due to his distinctive design innovations, most notably his inverted flame stitch pattern, which became one of his signature styles (fig. 32). As a Black boot maker working in Texas during the era of segregation, Lusk's extraordinary success and long list of celebrity clientele were notable. Lusk continued crafting boots until his passing in 1977.

Another important maker was Jack Reed, who also worked in Texas. He was famous for the precision of his work, but he was also famous for connecting people. He not only trained many boot makers still working today, such as Michael Anthony and Richard Cook, he also started the Boot and Saddle Makers Roundup. Held every year in Wichita Falls, Texas, this gathering provides an opportunity for boot and saddle makers to get together annually to exchange ideas and friendship.

As cowboy boots became increasingly embedded in performance, the demand for highly personal and often eye-catching footwear grew. Mid-century bespoke boot makers rose to meet this need, combining time-honored techniques with bold new designs that increasingly mirrored the ambitions of their wearers. Whether crafting boots for working ranch hands, rodeo stars, or rising entertainers, these artisans adapted to the evolving roles of the cowboy, negotiating the tension between function and display as well as tradition and innovation. Perhaps even more importantly, is that many of the makers taught the next generation, ensuring that industrial mass production did not overshadow the value of individual artistry and careful handwork. In this way, their legacy should not only be measured in the boots they crafted but also in the networks of knowledge they created. By ensuring that skills, stories, and techniques continued to be passed from one generation to the next and by instilling in young makers the confidence to reinterpret tradition in order to meet new demands, the work of these bespoke boot makers continues to shape the cowboy boot and ensure that it remains anchored in heritage, identity, artistry, and community.

Fig. 26: In 1911 boot maker Tony Lama established his business in El Paso, Texas. A photograph from 1939.

Fig. 27: At first Tony Lama repaired boots, but before long he turned to custom boot making. The company grew and by the 1930s was producing close to 40 pairs a day. After World War II, the company became a central player in the cowboy boot industry. This pair dates to the 1950s. Tony Lama, American, 1950s.

Fig. 28: In 1935, Acme Shoes, a children's footwear manufacturer, relocated to Tennessee and rebranded as Acme Boots. Founded by Jessel Cohn and his son Sidney, the company rapidly grew into one of the most prolific cowboy boot producers of the 20th century. This peewee exemplifies Acme's signature jewel-toned inlay designs. Acme Boots, American, 1940s–1950s.

Fig. 29: Charlie Dunn has been called the Michelangelo of cowboy boots. Dunn's true artistry, however, lay in the fit of his boots. He was famous for how carefully he took his measurements, ensuring a truly bespoke finished product. Charlie Dunn, American, before 1993. Collection of Texas Traditions.

Fig. 30: One of Charlie Dunn's most famous designs features blooming prickly pear cacti up the boot top embellished with a course of barbed wire run along the collar. This pair highlights Dunn's exceptional inlay and overlay work. Charlie Dunn, American, before 1933. Collection of Texas Traditions.

Fig. 31: Master boot maker Ray Jones was famous for making durable, elegant boots; his work retained crispness even after years of wear. He favored stitched boots with white beaded (piped) side seams, and his signature toe bug featured two "leaves" resembling a handlebar mustache. Ray Jones, American, before 1983. Collection of Adam Goeglein.

Fig. 32: One of Texan Willie Lusk's most distinctive design innovations was the flame stitch pattern. As one of the only Black boot makers working in Texas during an era of segregation, Lusk's extraordinary success and long list of celebrity clientele is notable. Willie Lusk, American, before 1976. Collection of Adam Goeglein.

Fig. 33: Following the master shoemaking tradition, Dunn took on an apprentice, Lee Miller, who has in turn become one of the most respected boot makers working today. In 1993, Miller made a pair of boots to honor Charlie Dunn's memory. As a special gift to the Bata Shoe Museum, Miller and his team recreated this special boot in black. Lee Miller, Texas Traditions, American, 2025. Generous gift of Lee Miller.

Wrangler

INTERVIEW WITH MASTER BOOT MAKER LEE MILLER

ELIZABETH SEMMELHACK: Let's start at the beginning. You are one of the most revered cowboy boot makers today. What got you into boot making?

LEE MILLER: Well, I grew up in Vermont. My mother was raised on a farm and she wore cowboy boots. My older brothers did too. I was born in 1954, and culturally cowboy boots were becoming popular when I was around ten. When you turned on the TV there would be Westerns—that's what you saw as a kid. You also have to remember all of the counterculture impact too, like the Beatles, the Rolling Stones and Crosby, Stills and Nash, everybody was wearing hiking boots and cowboy boots.

I always wanted to be an artist, and pursued that all through school. My fascination with cowboy boots and footwear in general came to me when I was eighteen. I was college prep, but when my mother asked, "What are you going to do?" I answered, "I want to learn how to make cowboy boots and hiking boots and shoes." Rather than telling me that I was crazy, she supported me. She asked, "How are you going to do this?" And I said I would try and find somebody locally who could teach me, and then I would go ahead and try and learn on my own. I wound up getting a job working for a local Italian shoe repairman in Rutland in 1972.

For the two years that I was working for him, I was also trying to learn how to make cowboy boots. I did make a pair of shoes, but they were absolutely horrible. Then when I was nineteen, I went to North Conway, New Hampshire, and tried to apply at a place making cross-country ski boots and hiking boots. I thought, okay, I've got the credentials to work here, but they only hired family. I didn't know what to do. The school that was the most popular for shoemaking at the time was in Lynn, Massachusetts, but the building had just burned down.

There was also a school in Altoona, Pennsylvania. I flew there, but it really wasn't for me. My high-school guidance counselor found a school in Oklahoma, affiliated with Oklahoma State University, that offered a two-year associate's degree in boot making program. They gave me some credits because I had prior experience, so I was able to complete it in a year and a half.

One of my fellow classmates was Randall Merrell. He graduated before me and was making cowboy boots and hiking boots in Vernal, Utah. When I graduated he said, "Hey, if you want a job, we'll make hiking boots and cowboy boots together." So I did that for a few years. It was in 1977 that I got a phone call from Charlie Dunn, who was looking for help here in Austin, Texas.

ES: Did you realize who he was?

LM: Oh, yeah. In 1974 my mother had died, and a friend of mine came to see me. He had recently traveled to Austin, Texas, and told me, "Hey, I've got to play you something." So we sat in his van in the driveway and he put in an 8-track tape and we listened to the song "Charlie Dunn," by Jerry Jeff Walker. I remember thinking to myself, "Oh, he's famous, and he's doing what I want to do, but of course I'll never be famous like him." That's how I first heard of Charlie. Then fast forward three years, and there I was working for him.

ES: When you went to school in Oklahoma, was the education focused only on hand shoemaking, or was the school also looking to prepare its students for industrial shoemaking?

LM: It was solely focused on all traditional, handmade cowboy boots. The teacher was an ex-Marine, and he really didn't like me. I mean, I had long hair. I was Yankee, and he didn't take me seriously at all. He resisted any attempts of getting me into the boot-making department. The school taught traditional cowboy boot making and traditional saddle making. My diploma says that I'm a saddle maker as well as a boot maker, but I'm not. Once I got in, I stayed in the boot-making department; I had no desire to learn how to make saddles. I did want to learn to make other kinds of footwear. I wanted to learn how to make hiking boots, but when I mentioned it to the instructor, it was like I had opened up a box of horrors. I was clearly upsetting the apple cart.

But he did allow me to do it—I made a pair of hiking boots. So I kept asking him to do things that he didn't want me to do. Like rather than using fabric for reinforcements, I wanted to learn the old ways of using leather. Everybody else was toeing the party line, and here I was getting him to show me things that he didn't want to show me. This continued on throughout the entire time I was there, asking him to show me things that people were not asking, but I did, I wanted to know.

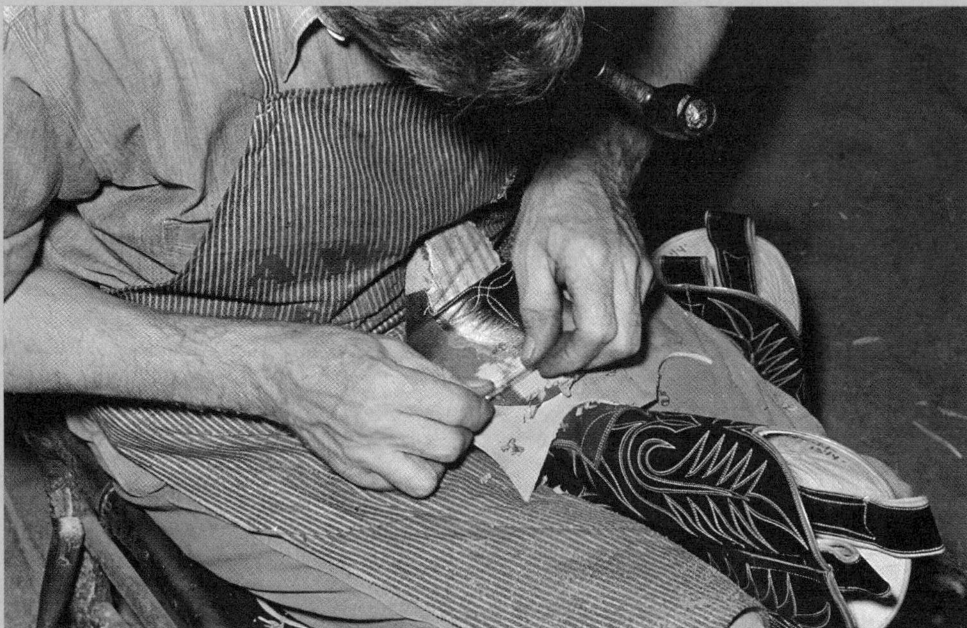

Roughening the leather of the lower part of the boot before attaching the upper with glue.

ES: You were asking him things that were about traditional craft, right?

LM: Yes, traditional boot making. I wanted to make two-piece boots, like a Wellington boot, and he was just really resistant for me learning anything. However, I have a picture of the last two pairs of boots I made while at the school. The two-piece pair I made for him.

ES: And? Did he like them?

LM: Oh, he loved them, yeah.

ES: How many students were there?

LM: There were about thirty students in my class. Some of them were women, people don't realize that women have been in cowboy boot making for a while. The class had people from lots of different backgrounds. There were ex-military, there were Native Americans, there were people there from all over the country—Illinois, Virginia, Kansas, Massachusetts. We were all there in one room learning how to make cowboy boots. It was really incredible just to meet everybody—the camaraderie. I am still in touch with a lot of the people that I went to school with.

For me, being from Vermont, seeing everything with my own eyes, just it kind of made me think, okay, do you really want to make hiking boots? No, cowboy boots are where it's at. So slowly over time, I just stopped wanting to do anything else but make cowboy boots.

ES: So what was the reason? Was it the opportunity for artistry? In comparison, hiking boots seem very practical!

LM: I fell in love with the West and what it represented, and the people I was with, and I just loved the culture.

ES: So what does the cowboy boot represent for you?

LM: Well, I mean, if you were to think about the people I was meeting, their rugged independence—they could do anything. It was also the mountains and the flatlands. It was the hauntingly beautiful culture of what the West was.

ES: It strikes me that you were approaching cowboy boot making from a similar stance; You were determined to do it, you took yourself to Oklahoma, you had the drive to learn all aspects of the craft. Is there a commonality there?

LM: Well, I never saw myself as a part of the West. I was an outsider, but it just kind of sucked me in. I became friends with bull riders and cowboys. I thought, I'm nothing like them, but I love what they represent, and I love what they do, and I love the culture.

ES: What happened after you graduated?

LM: I went to Utah and I worked with Randall Merrell, who went on to found the Merrell Footwear Company, which is huge today. I worked for him when it was just a one-man shop. He hired me, then he hired a friend of mine from Kansas, then he hired another friend of mine from Chicago. And we were all from the same school, and we were all working for him up there in Utah, and it was just an absolutely wonderful time. I even got to go on some cattle drives.

Fitting upper to lower part of the boot top at a cowboy bootmaking shop in Alpine, Texas. Russell Lee, 1939.

I met people who would go out elk hunting and bring me elk skin, and I would have to make cowboy boots out of their leather. So even though I was making hiking boots for Merrell, honestly, cowboy boots were where it was at for me.

After I left Randall Merrell's shop, I moved to a small town near there called Roosevelt, in Utah. A doctor from a Native American reservation had said to me, "Hey, you can live in my house, and we'll play in the jazz band together, and you can run the shop in Roosevelt." So that's what I was doing, running a shoe repair shop and playing in a jazz band in the evenings. Then one day in November of 1977 I got in a fight. The sheriff of that small town came in and kind of picked a fight with me. And then my boss at the time, who was a New Yorker, sided with the sheriff. So there I was being told what to do, and I didn't like it, so I basically either quit or was fired, and I didn't know which it was, but I acted in such a manner that I could never go back. And so then I went back to the reservation, I was sitting in my room at the doctor's house on the hill going, okay, what am I going to do now? I don't have a job. The only job I had is gone. And then there was a knock on the door, and it was the doctor's wife, and she said, "Lee, you have a phone call." I said, "What? I don't even have a phone." And it was Charlie Dunn's shop offering me a job. And I went and I grabbed the phone, and they were giving me a chance to work for Charlie, they were going to pay me pretty good money with benefits, and so there was no way I could say no. And I flew down from Utah to Austin, and that was the beginning of my time here.

ES: That is incredible timing!

LM: So that's how that really happened. It was just so weird. Apparently they had been looking for me for four months. When they finally found me, they called me that day. When I met Charlie, the first thing he said to me was, "Where are you from?" You have to remember, I was twenty-three and he was seventy-nine. I said, "Well, I'm from Vermont, Charlie." He said, "Vermont?" he said, "Well, isn't that where all the vermin are from?" And I said, "Well, I don't know, Charlie, I guess." And he says, "Well, you're a damn Yankee," and I said, "Yeah?" And he said, "Well, do you know what the difference between a Yankee and a damn Yankee is, Lee?" And I said, "No." He said, "Well, a Yankee will come to Texas and then he'll go home, but a damn Yankee will come and he'll stay. So you're a damn Yankee." And I said, "Okay, Charlie," because to me, he was Picasso, and I was just a twenty-three-year-old fresh off the plane from Utah.

I was in the presence of a giant. He was 135 pounds, 5'7", maybe 5'6", wearing a beret, and I was in awe, completely in awe. But I was very lucky, Elizabeth,

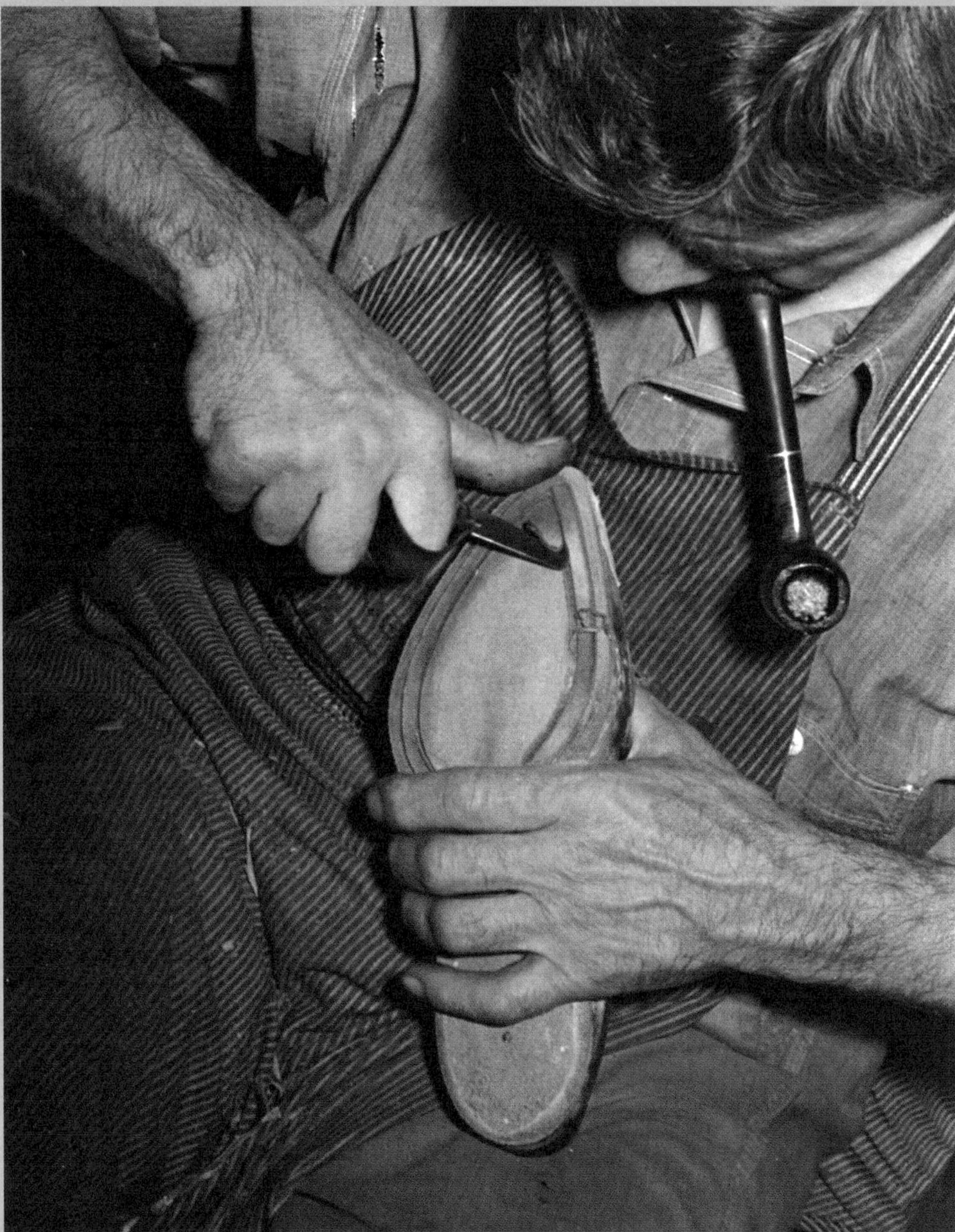

Preparing the sole of a cowboy boot to be welted at a cowboy boot-making shop in Alpine, Texas. Russell Lee, 1939.

because he had a shop full of warm boot makers from Mexico who embraced me and helped me became a part of the shop. It was a wonderful time.

ES: How many people did Charlie Dunn employ at the time?

LM: Well, let me see, there was Charlie, and there were about three other Mexican boot makers. There was also one White guy from Albany, New York, who I ended up training. That was it at the time, but it grew. The guy from Kansas who had been working with me in Utah eventually came to work for Charlie. I remember a guy showing up from Chihuahua, Mexico, he was an older boot maker, and spoke no English. Charlie told me that I was going to be his boss, but I said, "Well, Charlie, I don't speak Spanish." And he said one word to me, "Learn," and then he turned around and he walked away.

ES: Did you?

LM: Yes, the other people working for Charlie took pity on me and said, "Okay, we're going to teach you every day. We're going to listen to the Mexican radio. We're going to teach you new words every day." And so over a period of years, I did learn how to speak Spanish.

Even more importantly, what I learned from learning Spanish, was that the Mexican boot makers really embraced me and began to share the secrets of their boot making with me. So at the same time that I was learning from Charlie, I was also learning from them. What I loved about working with Charlie was that I could ask him anything. I could say, “Charlie, tell me the first stitch pattern you ever saw,” and because he was born in 1898 and grew up making cowboy boots, he could tell me these things.

So I found that it was like working for history, and I love history. So I was able to find out what it was like to be a boot maker in 1920, what the tools were that they were using and what their lives were like. It was an incredible opportunity to work for him and to hear these stories firsthand from him, somebody who had lived and breathed cowboy boot making his whole life. He taught me how to draw—he was a much better artist than me. He taught me his secrets.

ES: And when you first started working for him, was it like a traditional shoemaker shop, you were doing a portion of the work?

LM: Yes, I was considered the bottom person. So the bottom person would take the fancy uppers, trim the insoles, lash them, toe box them, build the soles and heels, and then finish the boots. That was my job. Eventually, Charlie gave me the unique ability to move around. I guess he liked me. He would say, “Okay, you can make tops. You can help me draw stitch patterns. You can measure customers.” He allowed me the chance to move out of that position and to do other things. Nobody else really got that opportunity.

Are you familiar with the photographer Russell Lee? He was hired by the US government in 1937 to travel the Southwest, and to take pictures of people doing traditional things. He went to Alpine, Texas. If you look at those things, holy Toledo, what a treasure trove.

I guess what was happening at that time was that Mexican boot makers were settling in Central Texas—San Antonio, Austin—bringing their cowboy boot-making skill. Then you had the Germans, the Polish, the Czechoslovakians, Charlie was Irish, and everyone's skills were merging, helping to create the cowboy boot as we now know it.

ES: I have thought a lot about the impact of this amalgamation and am very interested in why things emerge when they do. One of the things that I've thought about, in looking at some of the inlay work, is the potential influence of Russian, Balkan, and Crimean leather work on cowboy boot making. There's a lot of visual similarity there.

LM: Absolutely. You can see where things might have come from, but by golly, Mexican boot makers also added their own influence. Which made everything ever so glorious, the techniques that they brought, which no one had seen. This flourish basically came from Europe, Spain, and made its way to Mexico, and then came up from Mexico and Central Texas.

ES: Now I have another question, how did the toe flower start? Was it first structural and then become the signature?

LM: The toe flower—we call it a toe flower; in Oklahoma, they call it a toe bug—is a structural element. There is a famous story about Enid Justin and the toe flower. During World War II she battled the US government to allow her to keep doing the toe flower. During the war the government was trying to stop anything considered wasteful or unnecessary in shoe construction, but Enid argued that the toe flower was a structural element. So it is structural, but it's also decorative.

ES: Right, those things definitely do not have to be in opposition to each other. Switching gears a bit, of the boots that you've created—you were talking about the two-piece, the Wellington that you made in Oklahoma—do you have other boots in your own personal history that they stand out for you as stepping stones or highlights for what you were able to achieve?

LM: I guess. I mean, I made a lot of boots in Oklahoma, I made a lot of boots in Utah. Slowly, I learned how to get better at it, but I really didn't learn how to make really good boots until I got here. I have my early boots that were made here, and you could actually see the genesis of how my tastes changed. So in other words, the first pair I ever made were completely plain. They had stovepipe tops and were plain. Then, slowly, the toes became more pointed and I began to do decorative stitching. As a boot maker, I will say this to you, a lot of customers are drawn to inlay work, but fancy stitching is much more difficult to do (fig. 33). But, ultimately, I start with the silhouette. Our boots, I don't care if they're fancy or plain, they've got to have a beautiful silhouette. That is the most important thing, they have to have a beautiful silhouette.

RHINE-STONE

The cowboy, ever a creature of the modern age, kept evolving alongside new technologies that were shaping his image and meaning. Just as the advent of film had transformed the cowboy into a moral, heroic, and distinctly White icon, radio introduced a new dimension to his mythology: the cowboy as singer and storyteller (fig. 1).

SINGING COWBOYS

Before radio, American music varied by region. Urban centers fostered genres such as ragtime and jazz pioneered by Black musicians, while in the South, the blend of Anglo-Celtic and Black musical traditions featuring guitar, banjo, and fiddles combined to create what was termed "hillbilly" or "country" music. Out West, the music of cowboys intermingled with Mexican corridos and European polkas, as well as Indigenous musical influences, to create a distinct regional sound. Urban and rural American music, however, had image "problems." Jazz was linked to urban "degeneracy," an opinion dripping with overt racism, while country music was held to be uncouth and low-class, a view replete with classist prejudices and regional snobbery. Western music, in contrast, was centered around the unifying figure of the American cowboy and gained popularity nationwide.

The cowboy, alone on the range, guitar in hand, "stifling [his] longings for human companionship with song,"[63] was already an established trope long before the radio or "talkies" were invented. However, the release of the first sound film in 1927 gave the singing cowboy his voice. The first singing cowboy movie was the 1929 film *The Wagon Master*, starring Ken Maynard (fig. 2). Within short order, this new genre—dubbed "Horse Operas"—captured the public's imagination. The widespread appeal of this new type of singing hero inspired country musicians to align their more regional sound with the national popularity of the cowboy and to incorporate cowboy elements into their costuming. Jimmie Rodgers, known as the "Father of Country Music," provides a clear example. He rose to fame in the 1920s with his yodeling "hobo" sound, which he performed wearing brakeman's clothing. By 1929, however, he began to adopt more of a cowboy image, including wearing cowboy boots, and his fame grew. One of the most important developments in

Fig. 1: *Five Singing Cowboys*, 1920s.

bringing country and western music to a larger audience was the launch of 650 AM WSM in Nashville in 1925, followed soon after by its signature weekly program, the *Grand Ole Opry*. By 1932, the show was broadcasting nationwide and showcasing a wide range of country, folk, and western performers. While radio itself required no costuming, live performance did—and the stars of this era increasingly took the stage in dazzling cowboy attire.

SUPERSTAR

In the 1930s, one of the biggest box office draws was "The Singing Cowboy," Gene Autry, who helped define both the moral character and the fashion aesthetic of the archetype. Autry represented the "best" of America. He was always moral, kind, and was a man of action. He even codified these ideals into a personal creed—the "Cowboy Code"—which laid out the principles he believed every cowboy, and by extension every American, should follow:

1. The Cowboy must never shoot first, hit a smaller man, or take unfair advantage.
2. He must never go back on his word, or a trust confided in him.
3. He must always tell the truth.
4. He must be gentle with children, the elderly, and animals.
5. He must not advocate or possess racially or religiously intolerant ideas.
6. He must help people in distress.
7. He must be a good worker.
8. He must keep himself clean in thought, speech, action, and personal habits.
9. He must respect women, parents, and his nation's laws.
10. The Cowboy is a patriot.

Autry also *loved* boots (figs. 3 and 4). A 1938 newspaper article about him noted that "he has just one little mania that he indulges. He can't resist buying cowboy boots. He has a new pair made every time he sees some he likes. He has a dozen pairs."[64] But he did not simply collect—he wore them. Always. Even in unexpected settings. One journalist recalled meeting Autry for lunch and being stunned by his outfit: ten-gallon hat, a bright orange suit, and striking red cowboy boots.[65] In fact, reporters routinely remarked on his insistence on always wearing full cowboy costume including boots. Autry was an actor, not a cowboy, but his roles required commitment, and he never faltered. He knew what his fans wanted, and he obliged. Even when he joined the Army

Fig. 2: Ken Maynard in
Somewhere in Sonora, 1927.

Fig. 3: In 1939 a journalist interviewing Gene Autry noted that the star wore a ten-gallon hat, a bright orange suit, and red cowboy boots to their lunch meeting. Perhaps Autry was wearing this pair of Lucccheses in his collection. Lucchese, American, mid-20th century. Autry Museum of the American West, 91.221.137.

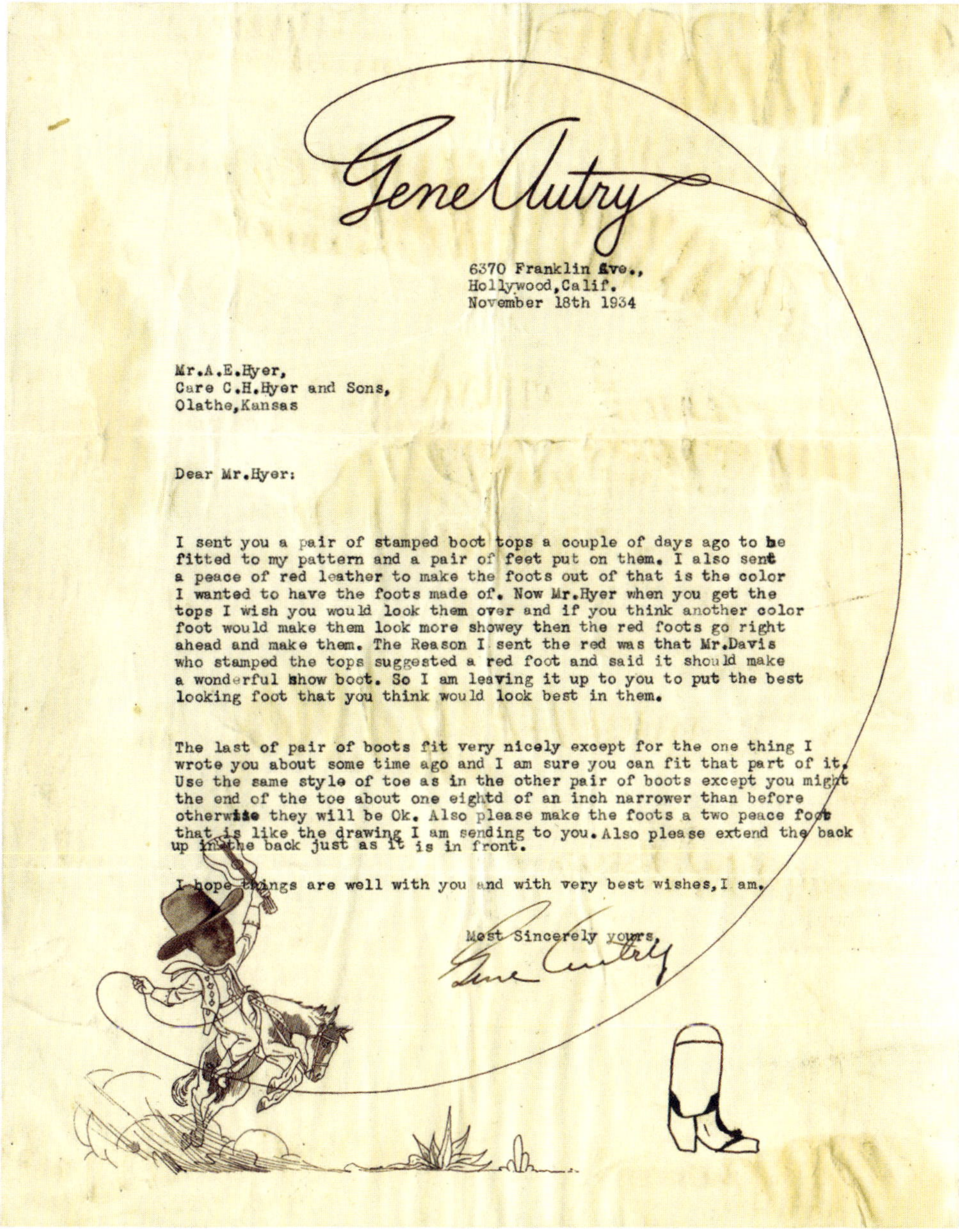

Gene Autry

6370 Franklin Ave.,
Hollywood,Calif.
November 18th 1934

Mr.A.E.Hyer,
Care C.H.Hyer and Sons,
Olathe,Kansas

Dear Mr.Hyer:

I sent you a pair of stamped boot tops a couple of days ago to be fitted to my pattern and a pair of feet put on them. I also sent a peace of red leather to make the foots out of that is the color I wanted to have the foots made of. Now Mr.Hyer when you get the tops I wish you would look them over and if you think another color foot would make them look more showey then the red foots go right ahead and make them. The Reason I sent the red was that Mr.Davis who stamped the tops suggested a red foot and said it should make a wonderful show boot. So I am leaving it up to you to put the best looking foot that you think would look best in them.

The last of pair of boots fit very nicely except for the one thing I wrote you about some time ago and I am sure you can fit that part of it. Use the same style of toe as in the other pair of boots except you might the end of the toe about one eightd of an inch narrower than before otherwise they will be Ok. Also please make the foots a two peace foot that is like the drawing I am sending to you. Also please extend the back up in the back just as it is in front.

I hope things are well with you and with very best wishes, I am.

Most Sincerely yours,

Gene Autry

Fig. 4, opposite: American singer and actor Gene Autry with his collection of cowboy boots, 1942.

Fig. 5: Letter from Gene Autry to Mr. Hyer, 1934. Collection of Hyer Boots Archives.

Air Forces during World War II, reports sent back to the States emphasized how much he missed his boots and that he felt a little uncomfortable in military footwear, wearing cowboy boots any chance he got.

Gene Autry wore boots made by a range of makers, including some of the oldest cowboy boot companies in America. The Hyer archives contains a letter from Autry asking for a new pair of boots to be made (fig. 5). He writes that he had enclosed stamped boot tops as well as the red leather he wanted for the uppers, explaining that he thought the color would make the "showiest boots," if Hyer agreed. Like many bespoke clients before him, he supplied the materials and dictated the details. Autry also asked for a few changes in fit and even provided a drawing showing how he wanted the vamp constructed. The Autry Museum of the American West in Los Angeles holds a number of boots worn by Autry in its collection and includes a range of makers. (fig. 6).

OLSEN-STELZER

Olsen-Stelzer is another legacy name in the history of the cowboy boot, founded in 1934 by two former Justin employees, Carl Olsen and Julius Stelzer. Olsen, originally from Norway, had

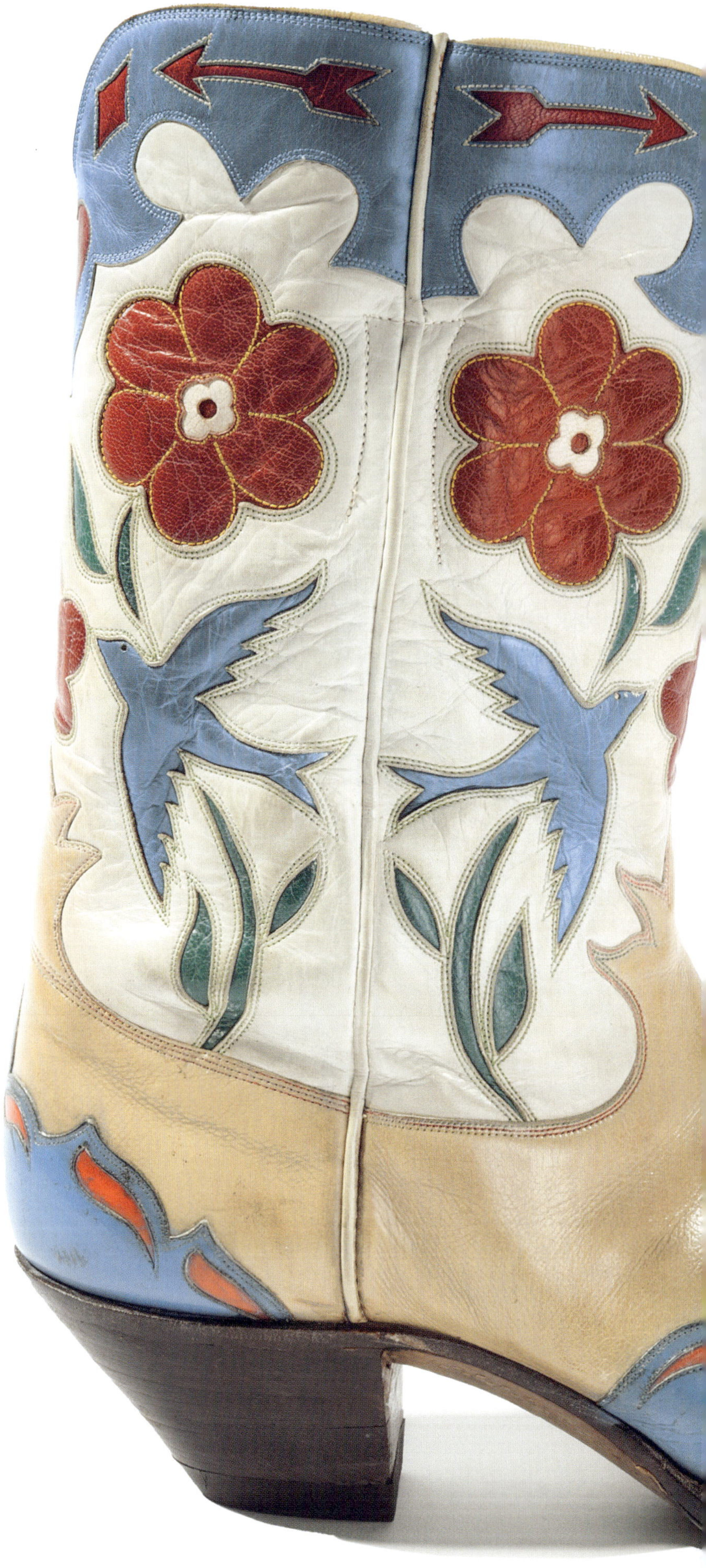

Fig. 6: This pair of Olsen-Stelzer boots in the iconic bluebird pattern was made for Gene Autry. Founded in 1934 by former Justin employees Carl Olsen and Julius Stelzer, the company became known for its highly decorative cowboy boots. With intricate inlays and bold designs, Olsen-Stelzer helped define the glamorous, show-stopping style of mid-century Western footwear. Olsen-Stelzer, American, mid-1930s. Autry Museum of the American West, 91.221.141.

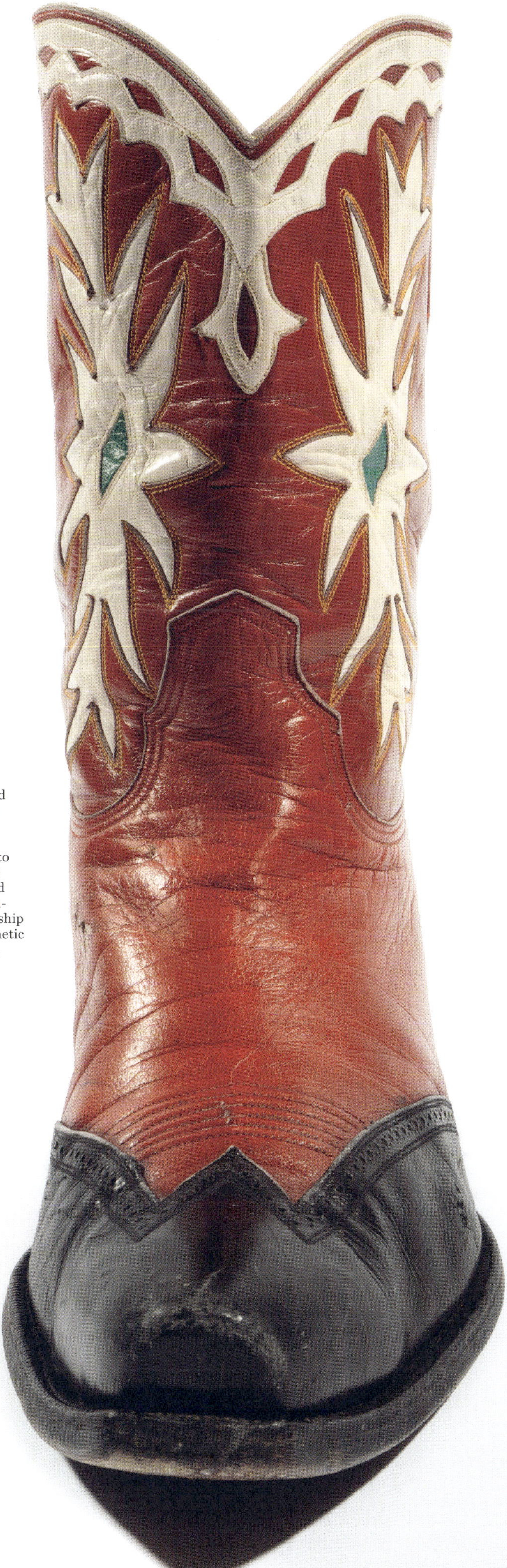

Fig. 7: Adolfo Romero and Ronnie Stewart founded Stewart-Romero Boot Company in Los Angeles in 1940, catering in part to Hollywood. This striking pair exemplifies their bold designs of the 1940s, combining refined craftsmanship with show-stopping aesthetic appeal. Stewart-Romero, American, early 1940s.

Fig. 8: This finely crafted pair of boots, likely made by Stewart-Romero, probably dates to just after World War II, when leather restrictions began to be lifted. The pattern of large blossoms and leaves is reminiscent of Renaissance textile. The use of gilded leather and thread further adds to the design's elegance, as does the use of subtly different red leathers. Probably Stewart-Romero, American, 1945–1950s.

Fig. 9: Actor and singer Dale Evans, c. 1945.

immigrated to Texas at the end of the nineteenth century and worked at Justin Boots before founding his own business in Henrietta in 1900. Thirty-four years later, he was joined by Julius Stelzer, the former production manager for Justin Boots and the former husband of Justin's daughter, Enid, who took over the business side of things. As capacity increased, Olsen-Stelzer became renowned for its decorative cowboy boots.

ROY ROGERS

With Autry off to war, Roy Rogers stepped into the spotlight and was soon crowned the "King of the Cowboys." Like Autry, Rogers also became famous for his colorful boots, but unlike Autry, Rogers had experience making shoes. Perhaps the work he did as a young man in a shoe factory gave him a deep appreciation of the craft. At his Studio City Ranger Trading Post, Rogers built a glass-enclosed boot-making department, allowing the public to watch cowboy boots being made right before their very eyes.[66]

BUTTERFLIES AND FLOWERS

The highly decorative boots favored by both Gene Autry and Roy Rogers reflected the larger shift in cowboy boot styling, with boots blossoming with birds, butterflies, eagles, and flowers as inlay and overlay techniques became more elaborate and refined during the 1930s and 1940s. Cowboy boots were now canvases for artistic expression. Sometimes boot makers created small stories through their work; other times, they used a seemingly disparate array of symbols that were more evocative than narrative. As the number of overlays and underlays increased so did the intricacy of the work. Tiny leather details rendered in a seemingly endless array of colors were cut and applied with precision, secured in place by the finest stitching. In the postwar period, metallic leathers would be added to the mix, along with embellishments like beads and rhinestones, pushing cowboy boot design even further.

Tooled leather was another decorative technique used on cowboy boots that flourished in the middle of the century. The craft was centuries old, but cut and skived [thin down the edges of leather where it will be joined to reduce bulk] leather for boots was impractical—it could not sustain hard wear or exposure to water—so it became a feature only of cowboy boots meant more for show than for hard labor, and the beauty of the work also required close inspection to be truly appreciated.

The symbolism found on decorated boots, be they appliquéd or tooled, often featured natural elements, but in the 1930s and 1940s embellishments increasingly referenced popular Wild West tropes. Longhorn cattle, cacti, and Texas stars were common motifs, as were playing card suits, gambling dice, and horseshoes—each evoking romanticized ideas of open-range risk, luck, and freedom.

There were also frequent allusions to the problematic "cowboy and Indian" theme so prevalent in media of the day. Arrows were especially popular, as were large eagles whose wings were stretched across entire boot tops. This style was marketed as "Thunderbird," appropriating a symbol sacred to many Indigenous cultures and reducing it to mere decoration, stripped of its spiritual meaning. This particular motif was so popular that Roy Rogers was reported to have thirty pairs of cowboy boots decorated with this symbol alone.[67] In some cases, these eagles were replaced by the profiles of egregiously stereotyped Indigenous men wearing feathered headdresses—imagery that reinforced the idea of Indigenous culture as a static relic of the past, rather than a vibrant and present part of contemporary life.

STEWART-ROMERO

With cowboy boots growing in popularity, new companies entered the fray. One of the most famous was Stewart-Romero (fig. 7). In 1940, Adolfo Romero and Ronnie Stewart founded their company, first in Mexico and later in Los Angeles, where they catered to Hollywood's growing appetite for stylish Western wear. Although their partnership was short-lived, ending in 1955, the boots they made represent some of the finest examples of mid-century boot making, celebrated for their exceptional craftsmanship and striking motifs (fig. 8).

CHEESECAKE

Although both men and women wore cowboy boots, they remained largely

Fig. 10: Roy Rogers wearing cowboy boots with eagle motif, 1948.

Fig. 11: This striking pair of boots features gilded stitching that shimmers like sparks against deep black shafts. The dramatic, tentacle-like overlay collar further adds to the bold design. However, if worn with pant legs covering the shafts, their brilliance would have remained a secret, appreciated only by the wearer—a perfect blend of showmanship and subtle luxury. American, 1930s–1940s.

coded as masculine, even as they became increasingly decorative. On women, cowboy boots appeared as costume, adding a sense of tomboyishness that was slightly transgressive but not radically so. They were clearly not being worn to do a job; instead, they were being worn to look "cute." A 1939 article from *Life* magazine illustrates how far things had shifted from the days of admiring skilled female trick riders. "One thing the rodeo has never had is sex appeal. Cowgirls, though glamorous in fiction, run to leather faces, legs like antique chairs and uncouth voices."[68] The article then goes on to praise "seven pretty girls . . . with figures cute enough to make hard-boiled New York sportswriters turn lyrical," noting that the women were not real cowgirls but rather "ranch debutantes" and their riding skills were "not really very good."

When shorts entered women's fashion in the 1930s, peewees in particular were seen to flatter the leg, and inspired the creation of lightly erotic "cheesecake" images showing women in cowboy boots and fringed skirts or culottes. In contrast to high-fashion sophisticates in spike heels, these images offered a version of distinctly American femininity that was rural, carefree, and, above all, playful. Dale Evans, famous as the wife and working partner of Roy Rogers, embodied this look in the 1940s (fig. 9).

SPARKLING PERFORMERS

The performativity seen in the "cowgirl" look found its match on the country music stage, where Western wear was also becoming increasingly spectacular. By the 1940s, country and western costumes began to rival cowboy boots, as rhinestones, spangles, and bold colors transformed the cowboy aesthetic into spectacle (figs. 10 and 11).

This transformation was driven by the work of a number of talented tailors, all from Eastern Europe. Rodeo Ben (Bernard Lichtenstein) in Philadelphia was the first, followed by Nathan Turk in Van Nuys, California, and then Nudie Cohn (Nuta Kotlyarenko), founder of Nudie Tailors in North Hollywood. Nudie, as Cohn was called, crafted complete outfits, including boots that were often embellished with rhinestones (figs. 12 and 14). It was a flashy look that also attracted other types of musicians. Just as country and western had blended, rock and roll began to enter the mix, and rockabilly performers, including Elvis Presley, also turned to these rodeo tailors and cowboy boot makers.

Fig. 12: Nudie Cohn on *The Jimmy Dean Show*, c. 1964.

Fig. 13: Country music star Patsy Cline, c. 1956.

Female performers were also dressed by these celebrated costumers. Patsy Cline often wore Nudie Cohn outfits head to toe, including her iconic white cowboy boots, a choice in keeping with the wider trend of women wearing white cowboy boots (fig. 13). As early as the 1930s, white cowboy boots were linked to female performance (fig. 15). In the postwar period, the trend grew more prevalent and was visually linked to the popularity of the white Hessians worn by majorettes (fig. 16). This tradition continues today in the Dallas Cowboy Cheerleader attire, which includes custom white Lucchese boots.

KID COWBOYS

As cowboy clothing became more costume than workwear, a burgeoning market for children's wear emerged in the 1930s and 1940s. Children were important audiences for cowboy movies, and many companies saw potential in the youth market. There was money to be made, but times were tough between the Depression and the war. A newspaper article from 1938 told the story of a terminally ill boy, Bobby Lee Wilkinson, who had been saving up for a pair of cowboy boots like the ones worn by Gene Autry, but as a last wish, he asked his mother to take his "nickels and pennies" and buy Autry a Christmas gift instead. She sent Autry a miniature pair of cowboy boots, which Autry later said was the most precious gift he ever received.[69] Between the lines of this poignant story lies evidence of a new market for cowboy-themed children's products. However, indulgences such as these would have to wait until the postwar boom to become widely commodified.

And what a boom it was. Production capabilities soared, and parents suddenly had disposable incomes that allowed them to indulge their children's Western fantasies, now stoked by a new deluge of Western movies and television shows as more and more families were able to afford television sets. Gene Autry, Hopalong Cassidy, Roy Rogers, and even the late Tom Mix all had branded children's boots (fig. 17). A *Life* magazine article on Hopalong Cassidy's wildly successful product endorsements provided insight into the broad appeal of cowboy-themed costuming, including boots. It even quotes famed cultural anthropologist Margaret Mead: "With fathers away from family life so much in modern times, mothers are afraid the boys will imitate them instead of their fathers, and turn into sissies; they encourage their little boys to copy the current play ideal of masculinity. Girls imitate the boys."[70] Certainly, the characters these stars played modeled ideal American behavior that inspired boys and girls, but perhaps the fact that some girls sought to be cowpunchers was itself a "problem."

TRUE GRIT

The crisis of masculinity suggested by Mead was not limited to concern about boys. The world was rapidly changing in the postwar years. Nine-to-five office jobs and single-family homes in the suburbs presented little opportunity to flout norms or test personal limits, and many men who had served in the war bristled under this new normal. Dreams of pulling oneself up by the bootstraps abounded, and the "true grit cowboy" emerged as the new cultural icon. In contrast to the singing cowboys and country-western performers, these actors did not wear fancy boots (figs. 18 and 19). Instead, their footwear more closely reflected what ranch hands wore in reality—brown, unadorned, and low-heeled. Their bravado was achieved through swagger and stoicism rather than surface decoration (fig. 20). Their characters continued to play by a "cowboy code," but the characters were often depicted as being pushed to the limits of their mettle

Fig. 14: As country music evolved, flashy suits with bold colors and rhinestones became standard for many performers. Their dazzling designs attracted not only country stars but also rockabilly musicians like Elvis Presley, blending Western style with rock and roll. Nudie Cohn created many of these costumes, including cowboy boots, and was himself quite a showman. This was one of his many personal pairs. Nudie Cohn Boots, American, mid-20th century. Collection of Jamie Nudie.

GODING

Fig. 15: Goding made cowboy boots for only a brief period, from the mid-1940s until 1969. This pair of peewees exemplifies mid-century design, though its strong use of gold makes it particularly dazzling. While some men wore white boots, most were made for women, including this pair. Goding Boots, American, mid-20th century.

Fig. 16: White cowboy boots have been associated with female performers since the 1930s. After World War II, their popularity grew, visually connecting them to the white Hessian boots worn by majorettes. This tradition continues today in the Dallas Cowboys Cheerleaders' signature look, which features custom white Lucchese boots. Laredo Boots, late 20th century.

Tom Mix
COWBOY BOOTS
OFFICE
BLACK SMI
LIVERY & FEED

Fig. 17: These Tom Mix boots for children were commercialized a decade after the actor's death. Although designed for small children, the prominent use of Tom Mix's name and image was most likely a marketing effort to attract the attention of adult purchasers nostalgic for their own childhood hero. The boots were well made and, this example suggests, much loved. American, 1950s.

Fig. 18: Ricky Nelson, John Wayne, and Dean Martin in *Rio Bravo*, 1959.

Fig. 19, opposite: John Wayne and Ricky Nelson in *Rio Bravo*, 1959.

and morality, making their decisions that much more hard-hitting.

Movie stars such as Gary Cooper, John Wayne, Jimmy Stewart, and Clint Eastwood epitomized this version of American masculinity on-screen. Their no-nonsense characters worked hard and made even harder choices—assuredly the country was working through the traumatic events of World War II.

Yet the overarching narrative in these productions remained clear—it was the good guys who reflected American values, but the fights required to get there were harder. An episode from the first season of the hit television show *The Rifleman* provides a typical example of the American morality that this media attempted to teach. The episode centers on an elegant Italian count who finds himself in the Rifleman's small Western town. His appearance and demeanor appear out of place, and he is instantly targeted by the town ruffians. The Rifleman's son is shocked by the treatment, and his father explains, "Someone who is strange or different is often treated with cruelty. Ignorance mostly, sometimes when people do not understand something, they think it is to be feared or hated. That is wrong, but it takes a long time to learn differently."[71] These words were delivered at a time when the world was headed into a period of long-needed change.

OPEN ROAD

For some, it was not morality that drew them to the cowboy but rather the ideals of freedom and self-determination. This was especially true for postwar bikers who took to the open road astride their motorized mounts in the 1950s. As with the cowboy, American bikers had their own sartorial uniforms, including footwear. In general, they favored engineer boots, which shared some characteristics with working cowboy boots (fig. 21). They were made of heavy, durable leather, with domed toes, low heels, and harness detailing. The behavior of many young bikers was also seen as echoing the moral ambiguity and outsider status of early cowboys in the Wild West. The mid-1950s films *The Wild One*, starring Marlon Brando, and *Rebel Without a Cause*, starring James Dean, helped further intertwine ideas of youthful alienation and cowboy culture.

CHANGE

As the 1960s dawned, freedom was on many people's minds. The civil rights movement, the women's rights movement, the American Indian movement, and the Stonewall rebellion all demanded that long-standing American values be reassessed, calling for freedom and equality for all—and some sought to incorporate the cowboy into these new dreams.

Before San Francisco became the locus of counterculture in the mid-1960s, a renovated saloon, christened the Red Dog Saloon, in Virginia City, Nevada, was an "outlaw enclave," where alternative living was expressed, in part, through nineteenth-century dress, including cowboy boots—a look epitomized by the saloon's folk-rock house band, The Charlatans (fig. 22).[72] The free-spirit narrative of the

HOTEL

Fig. 20: In the post-war era the "true grit cowboy," epitomized by John Wayne, became a rugged ideal. This pair was worn by the actor Robert Redford, who similarly portrayed characters embodying this nostalgic vision of masculinity. Lucchese, American, 1970s–1980s. Generous gift of Robert Redford.

Fig. 21: The biker culture that emerged in the late 1940s reflected an updated version of the cowboy ideals of freedom and self-determination. Like cowboys, bikers had their own uniforms and favored engineer boots in durable leather with domed toes, low heels, and harness details. American, mid-20th century.

Fig. 22: As the United States celebrated its bicentennial in 1976, reflections on pioneer life, the Old West, and the country's "frontier spirit" took centre stage. Cowboy boots became markers of this nostalgia and national pride. This pair, with its large embossed eagle, reflects the patriotic sentiment of the time. American, 1970s.

Fig. 23: Dennis Hopper, Peter Fonda, and Luke Askew in *Easy Rider*, 1969.

Fig. 24: In the 1970s, cowboy boots were increasingly becoming a part of fashion, especially for women. But rather than dressing like a cowboy head-to-toe, many wore boots to add Western flair to eclectic outfits. This pair reflects 1970s design while simultaneously recalling the curvilinear stitching found on cowboy boots a century earlier. Laramie Boots, American, 1970s.

hippie movement, like that of the biker gangs, was about fighting constraints and finding one's own way, and their eclectic outfits reflected this. The film *Easy Rider*, released in 1969, illustrated this fashionable blend perfectly (fig. 23). Instead of being one element of an entirely Western-themed outfit, the cowboy boot might be thrown into a sartorial mix that included clothing and accessories from other cultures and other eras. Leather crafts were highly regarded, and through this lens it is easy to see how cowboy boots and their history of craftsmanship found a place in this handmade aesthetic (figs. 22 and 24). Southern rock, which emerged out of this mix, added its own interpretation. The Allman Brothers and Lynyrd Skynyrd performed in clothing that flirted with the Western look, and they often completed their outfits with cowboy boots. However, by the 1960s, those interested in cowboy boots largely avoided the brilliantly colored styles seen in Horse Operas or the Grand Ole Opry. Instead, plain leather boots—subtly stitched or tooled, if decorated at all—became the standard (fig 25).

Amid this wave of cultural reckoning, the cowboy and what he stood for continued to be reconsidered. The 1969 film *Midnight Cowboy* offered a stark rethinking of the Western hero for a modern, urban world. Jon Voight's character, Joe Buck, arrives in New York City wearing a cowboy hat, fringed jacket, and fancy boots, believing his Western image will help him succeed as a hustler. Yet his costume functions less as a badge of strength than as a mask for vulnerability. The film recasts the cowboy as a figure of social alienation and sexual ambiguity, laying the groundwork for the queer reappropriation of cowboy iconography in the years that followed.

CONTRADICTIONS

As the 1960s moved into the 1970s, even more overtly political reasons for the cowboy boots' entry into broader fashion emerged. The American participation in Vietnam, and later the scandal of Watergate, had made the United States, in one writer's opinion, "an unpopular world power, [so] we started going back to our roots, in American history. Deep down, what could be more American than the cowboy?" In uncertain times, the cowboy and by extension his boots provided a kind of cultural shorthand that reassuringly linked national identity to mythic heroism.

Yet the politics of national pride were not the only meanings that cowboy boots

Fig. 25: The Charlatans have been frequently credited as the first 1960s San Francisco psychedelic rock band, as well as starting the Haight-Ashbury psychedelic scene. San Francisco, California, June 1966.

were given in these decades. In 1978, a Western-wear store owner in Oregon was asked what drove the revived interest in cowboy boots defining the decade. She responded that while cowboys hated hippies, cowboy boots reflected Mother Nature and being out in nature was something both groups could embrace. A customer in her shop put it more bluntly, saying they made him feel "macho." Such comments underscore the cowboy boots' versatility: they could stand for ecological simplicity, for traditional masculinity, or simply for rugged individualism.

Cowboy boots were even folded into a larger fashion trend toward unisex dress. Alongside jeans and Western shirts, they could be worn by men and women alike, signaling not only rebellion but also equality. Cowboy boots straddled a rare middle ground, appealing to both those nostalgic for the past and those eager to redefine the present.

In this way, cowboy boots continued to move beyond performance and be more fully integrated in dress more broadly. They appealed to many who grappled with the contradictions of the unsettling decades, and in doing so, continued to earn their place as enduring symbols of America (fig. 26).[75]

Fig. 26: Arguably one of the most famous cowboy boot makers of all time was Charlie Dunn. This pair, commissioned in 1983 for the wife of a Dallas lawyer, features his signature yellow leather roses, a technique he innovated. Charlie Dunn, American, 1983.

INTERVIEW WITH JAMIE NUDIE

ELIZABETH SEMMELHACK: Thank you, Jamie, for speaking to me about the history of your grandfather, famed rodeo tailor Nudie Cohn, and his work with cowboy boots. How did Nudie Cohn become one of the most famous tailors of Western wear in the world?

JAMIE NUDIE: It all started when my grandfather immigrated from Kyiv, Ukraine. He was eleven, and he ended up in New York City with his brother, Julius, who was eighteen. When my grandpa was still a young boy, he would go around and do odd jobs because he and his brother didn't really have any money. He would find a pair of shoes here, a pair of shoes there. Teachers would give him whatever they found and everything ended up being unmatched. He always said as he went further in his business that when he made it big, he would remember his humble beginnings. He wore unmatched boots to commemorate those times.

ES: That's great.

JN: I remember as a kid, he had all his boots lined up in his bedroom.

ES: How many pairs did he have?

JN: Maybe twenty. He would rotate them and then sometimes he'd gift them away. But my grandpa would have them all unmatched.

ES: As he was making clothing was he also making boots, or was he having boots made for him?

JN: Well, my great-grandfather was a boot maker, so my grandfather knew the ins and outs of shoemaking, but he was mainly focused on how to design and sew. There were seventeen people who worked in the store on Lankershim Boulevard in North Hollywood for more than fifty-one years. The store had all of the equipment needed to make boots. One of the things that my grandfather developed was the Nudie heel. It was a stacked heel.

When a customer would come in—when John Wayne came in—he'd sit down and they'd put the paper down on the floor and draw out his measurement. I remember as a kid watching this process. Then my grandpa would say, "Hey, do you want the boots to match your suit? Is it for a movie?" He would go over all the details. Cher was also one of his clients—she was a dear friend of his—and she had a pair of lizard-skin boots made. They had rabbit ears that went down the sides that snapped in place. Tex Williams was another celebrity client. He had one leg shorter than the other, so my grandpa would balance that out for him through the design of the boots.

ES: Many of the Nudie boots that I've seen are quite colorful, with rhinestones and other decorations often applied. Do you know when your grandfather first added rhinestones to cowboy boots?

JN: Well, the first rhinestone clothing we made was right when we started in 1947. For example, my grandfather had one client, Judy Lynn, who was called Miss Las Vegas, and she dressed in Nudie head to toe. Her boots were fully loaded with rhinestones. I have a pair of boots that belonged to my grandmother that have the rhinestone heels.

ES: Obviously, the designs your grandfather was making had a lot of decoration and a lot of color, and a number of men wore these pieces. Was there ever any discussion about "cowboys" stepping out in such grandeur?

JN: My grandfather would always say "real man wear rhinestones." These actors and musicians wanted [their attire] to be seen from the stage. Roy Rogers (fig. 2) was going to perform at Madison Square Garden, and he told my grandpa, "I want you to make my suit and boots and everything so the kid in the nosebleed section can see me."

Stuntman Dean Smith, who just recently passed, would talk to me about his friendship with my grandfather and how my grandpa would make boots and clothes for him. Dean would say, "Your grandfather always told me that real men wear rhinestones."

ES: I wonder if color film and TV had anything to do with that as well.

JN: From what I was told as a young girl growing up in the store, a lot of the color came from the colorful clothing worn back in Kyiv. This history played a big role in his design.

ES: Your grandfather often dressed people head to toe. Did he have any feelings about people mixing and matching?

JN: A lot of the rodeo queens, horse riders, and performers usually matched head to toe. But my grandfather also had people who would just come in for a pair of boots, and they didn't always have to be with rhinestones and embroidery. The customer might be a businessman wanting a plain black jacket or a plain pair of black boots. But always, the boots had to have that beautiful Nudie heel.

ES: What do you think the most ambitious costume he ever made was?

Fig. 1, p. 156: Robert Redford wearing a suit designed by Nudie Cohn in *The Electric Horseman*, 1979.

Fig. 2: Nudie Cohn flanked by Tex Williams, Gene Autry, Roy Rogers, and Rex Allen, c. 1960.

JN: The light-up suit worn by Robert Redford in *The Electric Horseman* (fig. 1). He would just collaborate and then figure out how to make it work.

ES: Did he always wear cowboy boots?

JN: Every day (fig. 3). In fact, he had one of the boot makers use the same plastic that he used to cover the seats in his Nudie automobiles to make him a long kind of wallet with inserts for his driver's license, credit cards, and money to wear inside his boots. So anytime we would go someplace, and it came time to pay, he would put his boot up against the table and then pull his wallet out. That's where he hid his money.

JN: He was an actual bootlegger [*laughs*]. You have mentioned that he often wore mismatched boots and that so many of his boots were colorful. Did he actually wear those colorful boots every day?

JN: Every day was unmatched. The only time that he ever wore matched boots was the day I got married in October 1980. I asked him if he could wear blue boots because he had a very beautiful blue suit with embroidered flowers on the lapel and stitching down at the bottom of the pants. He said, "OK, just this one time, I'll do it for you."

ES: Is there something that you would want people to know about your grandfather that we haven't discussed?

JN: He loved America. He used to tell me that his mother would tell him growing up, before they sent him over to the States, that the streets were lined with gold. She would say, "Go out there and do something with your life," which he did. A lot of his boots and suits featured the American flag and eagles (fig. 4).

ES: The fact that he ended up making Western wear, was this at all linked to his ideas of America?

JN: When he was in New York with his brother, Julius, they would go to the movie theaters to pass the time, and they would watch the westerns. My grandfather thought, even back then, that the costumes were missing something. Everything was a little boring.

He had been making G-strings for all the burlesque queens in the 1940s, and so he went to the musician Lefty Frizzell, who was one of the first to use rhinestones, just one *L* and one *F*, on his shirt. That's how he decided to get into Western wear. Everybody wanted to be a cowboy; it was the American dream. My grandpa even had horses. One of his friends was the cowboy actor and war hero Audie Murphy. They used to go horseback riding together. My grandpa would make him boots. Working with people like Audie Murphy made my grandpa feel like he had arrived at the streets of gold.

ES: Were Lefty Frizzell and Audie Murphy the first to wear Nudie designs?

JN: Tex Williams was another early client. My grandpa was determined to catch Tex's attention, so he went to Tex's house while Tex was mowing his lawn. My grandpa said, "Hey, I want to make you suits." And Tex said, "Well, I've heard about you on the street and that you're doing some good stuff." My grandfather told him that he needed money for a sewing machine before he could make him something. Tex responded, "Well, I don't really have any money. But I do have a horse out back. And I heard there's an auction in town. If we sell the horse, we can get the money for the sewing machine, and then you can make the clothing." So the horse was sold and the sewing machine was purchased, but then things went wrong. My grandpa and his young apprentice and the guys in Tex's band all got to drinking during the fitting. It is important to note here that my grandfather had borrowed the cloth to make the clothing on credit from the Linen House. When the outfits were done and he went to dress Tex and his band, the pant legs were like the length of the arms, and then the reverse—nothing fit. He had to remake everything. He went back to the Linen House to get more cloth, but the owner didn't want to advance him any more credit. My grandpa insisted that he wasn't going to leave until he got more cloth, and then finally at closing the owner agreed. Tex and the band looked great, played a sold-out show, and it took off from there.

My grandfather started making boots in the 1950s, the late '50s, and the rest is history.

Fig. 3: Nudie Cohn, c. 1970.

Fig. 4: Nudie Cohn boots at the Texas Country Music Hall of Fame and the Tex Ritter Museum in Carthage, Texas, 2015.

LET'S RODEO

RIGHT

By 1976, the cowboy was once again at the heart of national reflection. As the United States celebrated its bicentennial, nostalgia for pioneer life, the Old West, and the country's "frontier spirit" took center stage. But while the cowboy remained a beloved American icon, his meaning had changed.

SHIFTING SYMBOLISM

No longer just a symbol of grit and individualism, the cowboy was also becoming a marker of status, wealth, and political ideology. This was particularly evident in cowboy boots, which moved from functional workwear to luxury commodities, fashion statements, and revered artifacts of American folk art. Historian William W. Savage Jr., writing in the bicentennial year, captured the issues:

> Call it the preservation of heritage, call it nostalgia, call it what you will, it contains a fantastic amount of cowboy lore, either real or imagined, that offers a temporary psychological—sometimes physical—escape from the twentieth century somehow unnatural in its demands on body and soul. On one level, the cowboy is a symbol of chivalry, courage, honor and loyalty—virtues we wish were abroad in the land in greater profusion, virtues we know we ourselves possess and wish we could demonstrate for the general good. On another level, the cowboy is a symbol of all that we are not. He is colorful, decisive, active, glamorous, unfettered, exciting, uncommon, mobile, independent and confident. Like us, he moves through a world he did not make, but, unlike us, he can resolve his conflicts at their most fundamental levels and ride on, unmolested. That is to say the cowboy exists in a primordial state and may, accordingly, simply destroy his antagonists, if he cannot intimidate them into submission. We, in civilized societies, are unable to attain this ultimate resolution, maintaining order, as we do, through systems of intermediaries. But we buy cowboy hats and cowboy boots, and we pretend.[76]

Cowboys were included in many celebrations, and retailers were hopeful that this focus on "origin" would push the sale of cowboy boots. Sales did rise, and the places where cowboy boots were being sold and worn expanded across

Fig. 1: Canada West Shoe Company cowboy boots, late 1970s or early 1980s.

the United States. In an interview with Sam Lucchese in 1976, he reported that a longtime customer of his, a banker from Philadelphia, had called to let him know that he was now daring to wear his cowboy boots publicly in the East.[77] The article also noted that many men were seeking cowboy boots made from exotic skins and that they were willing to pay top dollar for them, going so far as to suggest that they had become true objects of desire. "What makes New Yorkers pay $200 to $1000 for a pair of cowboys? Deep in his heart, almost everyone had a yearning for something. . . . Some men would just like a fine pair of boots" (fig. 1).[78]

Yet, in many ways, the bicentennial was less about cowboys and more about settlers. Television shows like the long-running *Bonanza* and *The Virginian* were canceled in the early 1970s, replaced by shows such as *Little House on the Prairie* (fig. 2) and *The Waltons*. These shows reflected the changing times, such as telling the story of American expansion through the eyes of a girl, and many dealt with current topics through their slightly progressive narratives. But the fashions they inspired, such as the pairing of prairie-inspired clothing with cowboy boots, spoke to more conservative values.

DISCOS

The embrace of the cowboy boot—or more accurately, cowboy boot–inspired boots—in disco fashions took cowboy boots in a different direction, introducing them more broadly into fashion for the first time. These high fashion boots were not Texas made; instead, they were made in the fashion capitals of Italy or France. In 1977, *New York Magazine* touted *the* fashion item of the year as being $110 gilded leather cowboy boots by Italian designer Elio Fiorucci (fig. 3).[79] They embodied disco's maximalism, blending Western iconography with high-glam aesthetics. They also established that the cowboy look was now a high fashion option, one that contemporary fashion returns to again and again.

As disco culture flourished in the 1970s, cowboy boots found new life, not only on dance floors, but also in gay clubs, photo spreads, and subcultural fantasies. For many gay men, especially those coming of age in the wake of Stonewall, cowboy boots offered a way to inhabit—and queer—the rugged iconography of American masculinity. Leather culture, particularly in urban centers like San Francisco and New York, embraced the cowboy's silhouette: tight jeans, boots,

Fig. 2: Publicity shot from *Little House on the Prairie*, starring Michael Landon, Melissa Gilbert, Matthew Laborteaux, Melissa Sue Anderson, Linwood Boomer, Karen Grassle, and Lindsay and Sidney Greenbush, 1979.

Fig. 3: This pair of women's cowboy boots was made exclusively for fashion by the Edna in Toronto, Canada. Edna, Canadian, early 1980s.

Fig. 4: John Travolta tries on a pair of Tony Lama cowboy boots in *Urban Cowboy*, c. 1980.

and hats became part of an erotically charged costume that both subverted and celebrated traditional male roles.

One of the most influential figures in this aesthetic reclamation was Finnish artist Touko Laaksonen, better known as Tom of Finland. His exaggerated, hypermasculine characters—often clad in cowboy boots—transformed the cowboy into a gay sex symbol. Boots in his drawings were not just footwear; they were symbols of confidence, danger, and hypermasculinity. By the late 1970s, the cowboy had become a central figure in queer fashion and fantasy, turning the once-conservative icon into an emblem of gay pride.

URBAN COWBOYS

There were some people, however, who did want the "real" thing. In a 1979 issue of *The New Yorker* magazine, there was both a short article on brightly colored rubber cowboy boots for rainwear and an ad for a local cowboy boot shop run by Texans carrying Justin, Tony Lama, and Nocona boots. Widespread interest in authentic cowboy boots only increased the following year with the release of the movie *Urban Cowboy* (fig. 4). The film, starring John Travolta, who had most recently danced to fame in the disco-themed movie *Saturday Night Fever*, was based on an article written for *The Atlantic* about big-city cowboys in Houston and the Disneyesque

Fig. 5: A patron of Gilley's riding a mechanical bull, 1980.

Fig. 6: Dan Post Boots advertisement, 1980s.

honky-tonk bar, Gilley's, made popular by challenging times. As Aaron Latham writes, "America is confused about where it wants to go. And when America is confused, it turns to its most durable myth: the cowboy."[80]

But as Latham details, inside this vast establishment—Gilley's had a capacity of six thousand—people dressed in cowboy costumes were grasping at shadows from the past (fig. 5). The main focus of the article, Dew, wears a hard hat and sneakers by day, changing into his cowboy hat and boots only to go out after work when he tries to reaffirm his masculinity and place in the world by riding mechanical bulls. The honky-tonk trend and the *Urban Cowboy* movie led to increased sales of cowboy boots. Tony Lama, the company that made the boots worn by Travolta in the movie, saw a significant spike in sales (figs. 7 and 8). But as one wag noted, the majority of these boots would "never feel a stirrup or a rattlesnake's fangs," and they functioned as a "badge associated with an ideal."[81] What that ideal was, however, was about to be redefined.

Fig. 7: Interest in cowboy boots grew even more after the movie *Urban Cowboy* came out in 1980. John Travolta, the star of the film, wore this style of lizard wingtip boots. Tony Lama, American, 1980s.

Fig. 8: Starting in the 1970s, women's cowboy boots began to diverge more dramatically from men's styles. By the 1980s, wider shafts and deep V-shaped front lines became fashionable. The colorway of this pair echoes the famous style worn in *Urban Cowboy*, but its shape is less traditional and more fashionable. Justin Boots, American, 1980s.

Fig. 9: Ronald Reagan in *Law and Order*, 1953.

Fig. 10: Custom boots crafted for the 40th president of the United States, Ronald Reagan, featuring full quill ostrich and the presidential seal. Tony Lama, c. 1981.

SELF-MADE

The humiliation of the Vietnam War, the economic pain of the oil crisis, and years of social unrest had destabilized the nation's sense of self. Many aspects of the "cowboy code" were feeling outdated, too altruistic. The 1970s might have been the "Me" generation, but it was in the 1980s that individualism would take center stage, and conspicuous consumption came to define the era. The "true grit" ideals of the 1950s were retranslated into self-centered ambition, and profit was king. On the East Coast, the Wolves of Wall Street sported tasseled loafers and Rolexes,[82] while in Texas, oil tycoons wore designer suits with cowboy hats and expensive boots often made of pricey exotic skins (fig. 6).

THIN SKINNED

The use of exotic skins was not exactly new—snake and alligator had been used since at least the 1920s—but suddenly there was a call for shark, stingray, elephant, and anteater boots. The hide of the rare pangolin was so popular that in 1982, there were fears that the species would go extinct, with imports skyrocketing from zero in 1977 to 31,000 only three years later.[83] In the spirit of the day, Bill Powers of Justin Boots said that the company used only US government–approved skins and that, as far as they were concerned, "When you buy the pangolin, it's dead and gone."[84] With its distinctive patterned skin and price tag of around $1,000, pangolin boots certainly made a statement. Ironically, while these exotic-skin boots did good work proclaiming status, they were not usable on the range. These were delicate boots that likewise would "never feel a stirrup or a rattlesnake's fangs" (fig. 11).[85]

Oil wealth was at the center of this new look. "Black gold" had long been known to exist in Texas, but the boom began with

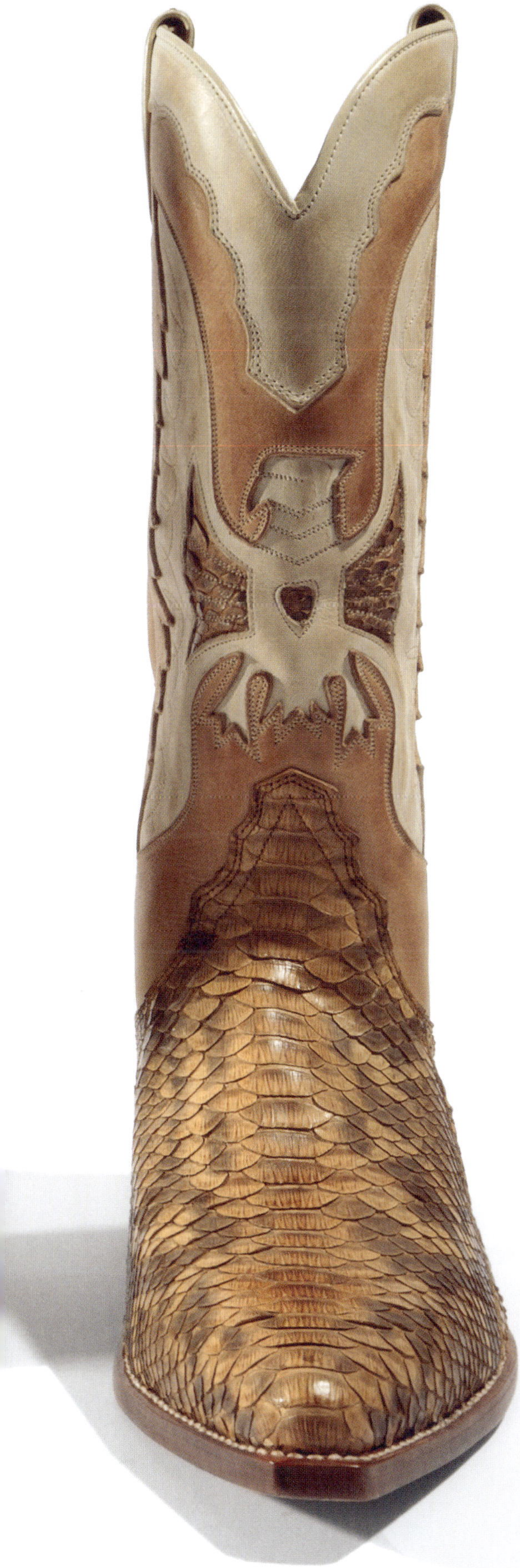

Fig. 11: Interest in cowboy boots made of exotic skins surged at the end of the 1970s and continued throughout the 1980s. This pair by Sancho Western Boots features python uppers with additional python embellishments on the boot tops. While exotic skin boots were effective for proclaiming status, they were too delicate for actual ranch work. Sancho Western Boots, Spain, 1980s. Collected by Stephen Pitch, generous gift of Anna Savoy.

the Spindletop strike in 1901. Although the supply and demand for oil ebbed and flowed throughout the first half of the twentieth century, the so-called black gold had the power to make men millionaires. The sudden wealth of what many thought were simple cowboys and farmers led to a wider range of characterizations, but the defining feature was a cowboy hat and cowboy boots. When *Time* magazine put multimillionaire "wildcatter" Glenn McCarthy on the cover in 1950, the illustration included a depiction of an oil derrick wearing a cowboy hat and cowboy boots. The article opened with this description of the man: "If it were possible to cap the human ego like a gas well, and to pipe off its more volatile by-products as fuel, Houston's multimillionaire wildcatter Glenn McCarthy could heat a city the size of Omaha with no help at all. Whether he would allow his rampant psyche to be dedicated completely to so prosaic a project, however, is doubtful—several million cubic feet would undoubtedly be diverted to a McCarthy Memorial Beacon which would nightly cast its glare as far west as El Paso."

This combination of oil wealth, greed, and cowboy iconography found its ultimate expression in the long-running television series *Dallas*, which debuted in 1978. J. R. Ewing, played by actor Larry Hagman, became the embodiment of the ruthless, larger-than-life Texas oilman. With his signature cowboy hat, boots, and swagger, J. R. Ewing represented a modern interpretation of the cowboy—one that stripped away the ideal of honor, embracing individualism purely for personal gain.

COWBOY PRESIDENT

While Texas oilmen continued to redefine the look of business in the late 1970s, Ronald Reagan was redefining the look of politics. Reagan started his career as an actor appearing as a "reel" cowboy in a number of Westerns. Immediately after the war, Reagan began casually to ranch, and when he became governor of California, he was often described as wearing cowboy attire. *The Washington Post* wrote about Reagan in 1967 that his "Western, television-cowboy look, carefully rumpled" came across as "all man. No mincing frills. Outdoors-y, athletic, earnest, he's the Marlboro Man."[86] Indeed, in his Western costuming Reagan embodied exactly what many Americans sought after years of social upheaval, an "authentic" hypermasculine leader who projected "traditional values" (fig. 9).

When Reagan was elected president in 1980, and throughout his two terms, he frequently wore cowboy boots, one of his favorite makers being Tony Lama. An article from 1984 described the delivery of four pairs of Tony Lama boots, normally $1,000 dollars each, but these had been customized with fourteen-karat gold presidential seals (fig. 10).[87] Reagan, however, was not the first president to wear cowboy boots: Teddy Roosevelt, Calvin Coolidge, Harry S. Truman, and Lyndon B. Johnson all wore them.

HISTORICAL PRECEDENT

Interest in cowboy boots continued to grow as the 1980s went on. Famed fashion editor Diana Vreeland's 1984 exhibition *Man and the Horse* at the Metropolitan Museum of Art in New York included an homage to the Wild West. Vreeland later recalled in the press how she had been given a pony by Buffalo Bill himself when she went to Wyoming at age twelve to escape a polio epidemic. Fashion designer Ralph Lauren, long associated with the Western look, sponsored the exhibition. The designer had been wearing cowboy boots since the 1970s, and in the 1980s, he focused much of his brand on the romance of the American West (fig. 13). His boots were more than fashion boots; they were made in the traditional manner, and he increasingly took inspiration from the more colorful and decorative styles of the 1930s and 1940s (fig. 14). When Tom Cruise wore a pair of brightly colored cowboy boots made by the company Champion Boots in the 1986 film *Top Gun*, a new era of decorative cowboy boots was born (fig. 12).

This renewed interest in cowboy boot styles from the 1930s and 1940s was mirrored in the neo-traditional movement in country and western music, which took inspiration from the likes of Hank Williams. An antidote to the "slick" country music preferred by urban cowboys, neo-traditional music hearkened back to earlier times, incorporating historic instrumentation and lyrical storytelling into its contemporary sound. Headliners included George Strait and Randy Travis, as well as a significant number of female performers. The Judds, k. d. lang, Shania Twain, and Reba McEntire all helped redefine country music's appeal, in part by wearing cowboy boots.

AMERICAN FOLK ART

Heritage brands continued to do well in this environment, and many revived historic styles and emphasized their long-standing legacies (fig. 15). One of

Fig. 12: Tom Cruise wore decorative cowboy boots as Lieutenant Pete "Maverick" Mitchell in *Top Gun*, 1986.

Fig. 13: Ralph Lauren embracing the Western aesthetic, 1979.

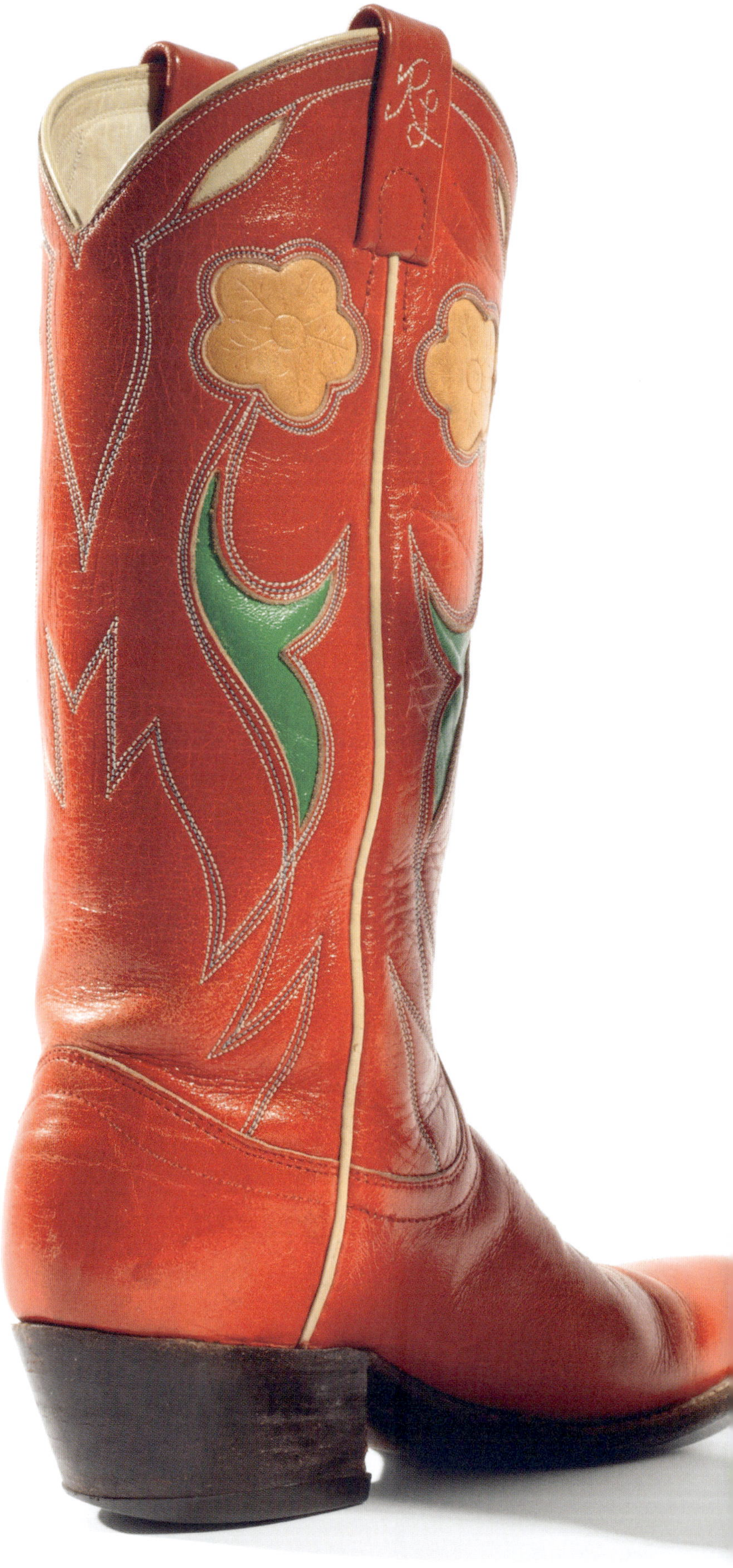

Fig. 14: This boot, known as the Selene, was released in 2020 as part of the fiftieth anniversary celebration of the Ralph Lauren brand. It was inspired by a Ralph Lauren boot from the 1980s, and was made with Lucchese. Ralph Lauren, American, 2020.

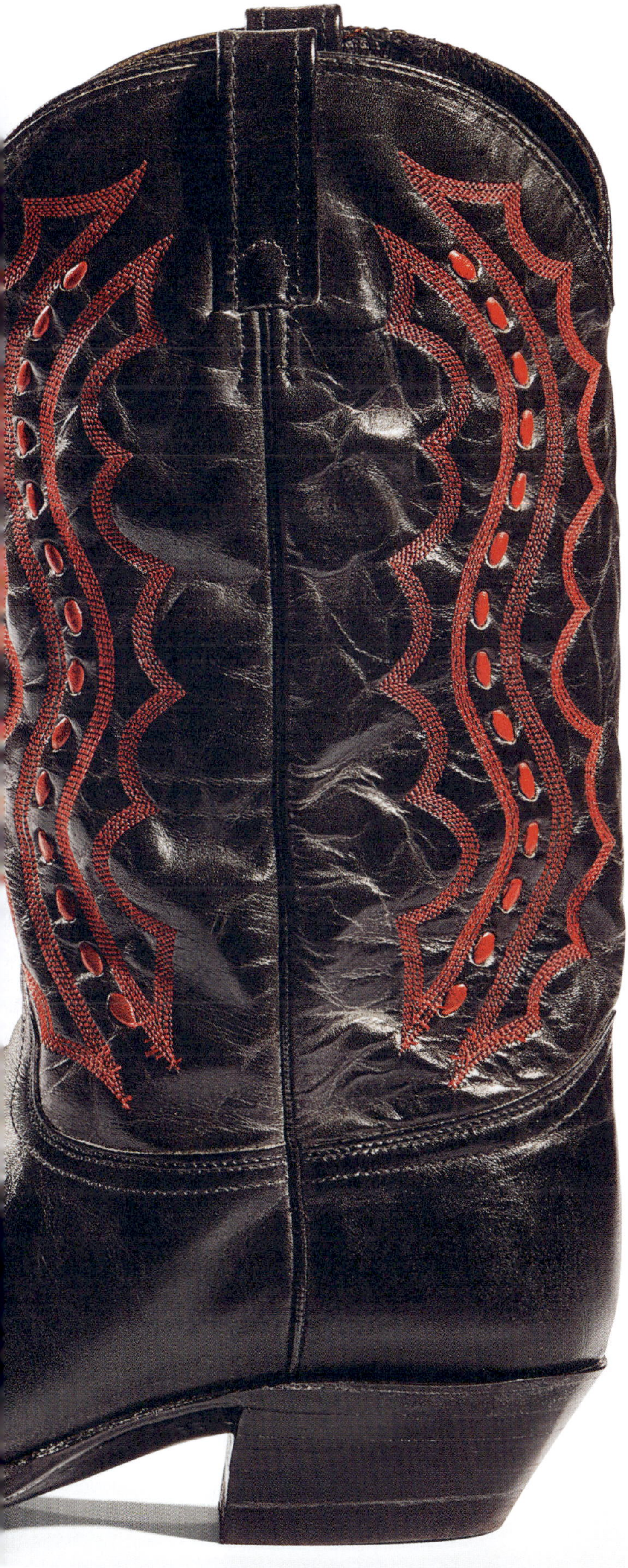

Fig. 15: These striking red and black boot were made by J. Chisholm Boots, American, 1990s. Collected by Stephen Pitch, generous gift of Anna Savoy.

those was Blucher Boots, which became Griffith-Blucher in the 1970s when cowboy boot maker Jay Griffith joined the company. Ever since its founding in 1915, Blucher Boots was renowned for the intricate overlay and inlay work found on its boots and in the 1970s, the company leaned into the moment. Griffith has been making boots since the 1930s, and he brought with him a deep appreciation of the history of cowboy boots. The famed folk musician and dedicated collector of cowboy boots Don McLean had a bespoke pair of Griffith-Blucher Boots made for him that beautifully navigated the intersection of heritage and contemporary style (fig. 16).

Paul Wheeler began making boots in 1947, and his son Dave took the craft as well. Wheeler Boots were legendary for making bespoke boots. Dave, in particular, was adventurous with his designs. The Wheeler's motto was that they did not make boots for people who needed them, they made boots for people who wanted them.

Rocketbuster Boots came on the scene in 1989 and was dedicated to making some of the most ornate boots available. Founder Marty Snortum wanted to bring vintage styles back and boldly reached out to Roy Rogers. As luck would have it, Rogers was very interested in reviving his old signature boots, and the two collaborated. After a few years, Nevena Christi married Snortum and joined the company. Her design skills took Rocketbuster Boots to the next level, and helped Rocketbuster merge contemporary with traditional sensibilities, drawing attention from fashion stylists to private collectors (fig. 17).

Montana Boots was another company dedicated to reproducing historic designs. In particular, the firm duplicated famous Olsen-Stelzer design styles such as the rerelease of Gene Autry's bluebird boots (fig. 18) and lace-top styles in both men's and women's sizes (fig. 19).[88] Their fidelity to historic patterns and materials greatly appealed to consumers eager to reconnect with earlier boot-making traditions.

Liberty Boots, started by Canadian Tony Benattar with Yan Ferry in 1993, leaned into the desire for decorative styles and offered boots inspired by historic patterns (fig. 20). As the company's renown grew, Liberty became more adventurous and began to experiment with an edgier look. Roiling skulls, sharp narrow toes, and perfectly proportioned under-slung heels began to define the Liberty aesthetic. Liberty's exceptionally well-crafted boots were made in León, Mexico (fig. 21). With the desire to always push the limits of design, Liberty also commissioned boots that featured *piteado* embroidery, a traditional form of Mexican embroidery done on leather using pita, a thread made from the agave plant. By the early 2000s, musicians musicians began to wear the firm's boots, but they were not just country stars, they were rock stars (fig. 22). In addition, Liberty offered bespoke boots that featured everything from tooled leather, inlay, overlay, and even rhinestones (fig. 23).

Another company doing extraordinary work that emerged in the 1990s was Tres Outlaws, based in El Paso, Texas. *Forbes* reported in 2006 that Tres Outlaws "once clocked a customer for $75,000 for a pair [of boots] whose mind-boggling design traced the history of Mexico, including $18,000 worth of gold and silver coins from various historical eras. The design alone took 100 hours, the hand-carving another 300 hours, and the color and dye work an additional 200 hours."[89] This work was assuredly done by master boot maker Scott Emmerich.

This new pinnacle for the craft irrefutably established cowboy boots as luxury objects, and more makers entered the field. One of these was Arditti, founded by Tomasso Arditti, specialized in boots made of exotic skins (pp. 232–33). Arditti even went so far to offer boots hand-carved by legendary tooler Jim Resley and embellished with real gold and palladium.

The revived interest in historic cowboy boots led to a reassessment of this American folk art, and suddenly, vintage cowboy boots became the focus of many collectors. Tyler Beard's classic book, *The Cowboy Boot Book*, published in 1992, was central to opening many people's eyes to the undeniable art of the cowboy boot. Within its pages, the most beautiful boots ever made could be ogled. Many bespoke boot makers today credit his work with inspiring them to pursue the craft, and many of their customers credit him as well.

At the end of the century, a new golden age of the cowboy boot was dawning. The apprentices of the mid-century masters were stepping into their own, new makers were entering the craft, and collectors and consumers were eager to buy. Cowboy boots could now be art objects, items of fashion as well as work wear, and in each setting maintained their importance as cultural signifiers. As the meanings given to cowboy boots became increasingly fluid, their target audience expanded.

Fig. 16: The 1980s revival of earlier cowboy boot styles mirrored the neo-traditional movement in country music, which also drew from the past. Heritage brands thrived in this climate, often reissuing vintage styles. Blucher Boots, long renowned for intricate inlays, crafted this bespoke pair for folk musician Don McLean, blending legacy craftsmanship with contemporary flair. Griffith-Blucher Boots, American, 1980s.

Fig. 17: Bespoke Rocketbuster Boots featuring peacock imagery made for Don Knobler, the eccentric Dallas Mavericks superfan, who famously wore his custom cowboy boots courtside to games. Rocketbuster, American, 2010s.

Fig. 18: In the 1980s and 1990s some boot makers began reissuing historic designs. One of those companies was Montana Boots which began reproducing famous Olsen-Stelzer designs styles from the 1930s and 1940s. This pair is a reproduction of Gene Autry's bluebird boots. Montana Boots, American, late 20th century.

Fig. 19: Other Olsen-Stelzer designs that Montana reintroduced included these "lace top" boots which they offered in both men's and women's sizes. After years of men being limited to "rugged" boots, these highly decorative styles were appealing to many. Montana Boots, American, late 20th century.

Fig. 20: Liberty Boots, started by Canadian Tony Benattar with Yan Ferry in 1993, leaned into bold, decorative styles inspired by historic patterns. Canadian-designed, Mexican-made pair of Liberty Boot Co., Sunflower model, early 2000s. Generous gift of Tony Benattar.

Fig. 21: These exceptionally well-crafted Liberty Boots were made in Leon, Mexico. Liberty Boot Co., *Killaz*, Canadian-designed, Mexican-made, early 2000s. Generous gift of Tony Benattar.

P17.66A
LIBERTY
BOOT CO.

Fig. 22: This boot design was named after Lefty Frizzell. The Liberty label features a cowboy so happy he is doing a back flip. Liberty Boot Co, *Lefty*, Canadian-designed, Mexican, early 2000s. Generous gift of Tony Benattar.

Fig. 23: The crisp look and inventive designs of Liberty Boots attracted an edgier crowd which included rock stars as well as country musicians. Liberty Boot Co., *Rock 'n Roll Heart*, Canadian-designed, Mexican-made, 2005-2008. Generous gift of Tony Benattar.

Fig. 1: Model Tatjana Patitz sitting on a bay horse wearing a long riding coat by Ralph Lauren Roughwear in Wyoming, 1989.

RALPH LAUREN AND THE MYTH OF THE WEST: COMMODIFYING AMERICA

Nishi Bassi

Fashion designer Ralph Lauren is often celebrated as a pioneer of American style. Much of his success can be attributed to his ability to create and market romantic, idealized fantasies of traditional American life (fig. 1). Lauren has sold multiple versions of "Americana"—both refined and rugged—since the 1970s. The more refined fashions include preppy clothing evocative of east coast elites who dressed for leisure activities, including boating, tennis, and horseback riding. At the same time, Lauren found success designing prairie skirts and dresses reminiscent of an age of westward expansionism, as well as rugged cowboy clothing and boots that embodied individualism and grit; tenets that were central to ideas of American nationalism in the latter half of the twentieth century.

Lauren debuted the Ralph Lauren Western and Polo Western fashion lines in 1978, selling plaid shirts, Southwestern prints, fringed jackets, and accessories made of tooled leather in the "spirit of the West." Lauren frequently employed nostalgia and ideas of individualism, ruggedness, and adventure—often defined as uniquely American traits—in his marketing. His print advertisements featured sweeping landscapes and open fields populated with horses, barrels of hay, and cacti. An ad for Chaps cologne from 1986 depicts a man with his son in historicized clothing standing in front of a tent and described as "living without boundaries." Another from 1988 summarizes Lauren's marketing strategy well:

> The West has always reflected the spirit of the American man. It represents self-reliance, strength, pride and a romantic vision of life. It is an image of a man at his most individual, most independent. . . . Chaps by Ralph Lauren. For the Spirit of the West that's inside every man.

Lauren's ads from this period often featured narrow and problematic representations of the ideal, "traditional" American family, namely White, heteronormative, able-bodied, and, often, upper middle class (fig. 2). Indeed, Lauren's "cowboy" did not reflect the diversity of the historic vaquero or cowherder, but remained a highly privileged figure who could move seamlessly between wide-open fields and expansive tennis courts. In 1985 a journalist for *The New York Times* described Lauren's advertisements as "propaganda posters for the nuclear family and the American Way of Life. They often depict rugged individualists . . . standing ready in their simple $260 sweaters to defend home, family and country club."

Advertisements for Lauren's Rough Wear line from the 1980s describe the clothing as "made to be worn." This collection featured painted leather skirts, deerskin trousers, and knitwear inspired by Navajo blankets. Depicted on young White models, these elements of Indigenous fashion were problematically rendered "American" and were central to the image of an ideal, and ultimately exclusionary, national identity that Lauren was selling.

In addition to his deft ability to create and sell a fantasy, Lauren's commercial success can also be attributed to a number of larger cultural changes taking place in American society in the 1980s. Under President Ronald Reagan's administration, there was an increased focus on nationalism and identity formation, as he sought to strengthen American foreign policy against communist threats. Reagan frequently used the image of the cowboy as a representation of the values his administration favored through its policies—strength, individualism, autonomy, and aggression—cementing this figure in the national consciousness.

At the same time, the cowboy was also enjoying a revival in pop culture. Western films, including *Bronco Billy* and *Wild Times*, and television shows, such as *Dallas* and *Little House on the Prairie*, also inspired cowboy-themed fashion and cowboy-inspired living. In 1982, *The New York Times* noted, "the demand for Western apparel created a $5 billion industry." In 1989, *Vogue* produced a multi-page spread titled "Fashion: True West." This article depicted models in Ralph Lauren clothing and noted the increased popularity of dude ranches for adventure-seeking travelers who were weary of big cities: "The American dude ranch has such mythic appeal that some vacationers fly in from Zurich just to 'round up the herd' and 'muck the stalls.'" It is clear that over the course of the decade, the cowboy remained both fashionable and increasingly emblematic of American identity, both in and outside of the United States.

The 1980s was also a period in which shopping was highly valued and celebrated as central to modern life, evidenced by the innumerable malls that were built across North America and the increasing numbers of fashion catalogues available for consumers. Identity formation, status, and self-improvement were increasingly linked to fashion consumption. Both the popularity of the cowboy and a growing focus on spending meant that there was a large consumer base receptive to Lauren's many Western lines.

Lauren often fashioned himself as a modern cowboy, wearing worn-out denim, polo shirts, suede hats, and Western boots. In 1982, he famously purchased a 16,000-acre ranch in Colorado. His embodiment of his own brand added a layer of authenticity and accessibility to his name. In many ways, Lauren became the romanticized figure that he sold through his work—someone from a modest background who had achieved enormous success by "pulling themselves up by their bootstraps." He represented the American dream: a young man from humble beginnings who became a billionaire through grit and determination.

Lauren's preoccupation with tradition and heritage is reflected in the boots he produced. In the late 1970s and 1980s, many fashionable, cowboy-inspired boots flooded the market from brands including Charles Jourdan and Andrea Pfister. However, Lauren's boots from this period resembled the "classic" cowboy boot style from the 1950s. Extant examples are minimally embellished and feature stitching and appliqué-work common to "traditional-style" boots. Made of high quality leathers, these examples were stylish, but also hardwearing and functional. In recent years, heritage bootmaking brands Lucchese and Rios of Mercedes have produced footwear for Lauren's brand, adding a further layer of authenticity.

Ultimately, the reason Ralph Lauren experienced so much success with Western wear is that his brand commodified traits that were central to the myth of the cowboy: nostalgia, individualism, and nationalism. By tapping into these deeply ingrained cultural symbols, Lauren not only shaped the aesthetic of Western wear but also reinforced its association with American ideals more broadly.

Fig. 2: *Spirit of the Prairie*, Ralph Lauren, 1989.

RE-CLAIMED

The twenty-first century ushered in a new era of reckoning with the mythology of the American West. The cowboy, long romanticized as a singular rugged figure, was being reconsidered in more inclusive ways—ways that acknowledged the diverse histories of those who shaped the frontier. The same was true for the cowboy boot, which was increasingly a medium of self-expression, a statement of identity, and a canvas for reinterpretation. Yet concerns continued to be voiced about who had the "right" to wear them.

BOOT MAK(HERS)

Women, for example, had always been a central part of cowboy boot making—the decorative stitching on boot shafts was often done by women; making complete boots was another story. The reasons given varied, the most common being that women were not physically strong enough to build entire boots, but this has proved false. Another reason stems from the history of shoemaking as a very gendered craft. In some cultures, it is women's work; in the West, it has long been considered a man's job.

Enid Justin founded Nocona boots in 1925, and while she had stitched boot tops for her father, she never made a pair herself. It was Melody Dawkins who, in 1980, became the first woman to own her own boot-making shop. Dawkins was a fifth-generation maker in a long line of cobblers.[90] She already had her own shoe repair store when she decided to learn custom boot making at the famed Oklahoma State Technical Institute.[91] She then became a custom boot maker famous for her detail and fit.

Dawkins was followed by Deana McGuffin, a third-generation New Mexico master boot maker, who learned boot making directly from her father, L. W. McGuffin, as an apprentice in 1982. At first, her father was not sure she had the physical strength to complete a pair of handmade boots, but she convinced him to teach her anyway.[92] After three years, she opened her own shop, becoming renowned for her exceptional work. The artistry of the cowboy boot is the focus of her work. Her most famous design is her Day of the Dead boots, which feature exceptionally intricate inlay and overlay work that takes over a hundred hours to complete. Like many master boot makers, McGuffin has long been firmly committed to keeping the craft alive by

Fig. 1: Lisa Sorrell, one of the most famous bespoke boot makers today, creates boots distinguished by intricate inlay and overlay designs. Each pair she makes is named after a song that has inspired her. Sorrell Custom Boots, *Working Man Blues*, American, 2014. Collection of Lisa Sorrell.

Fig. 2: For Sarah Madeleine T. Guerin, cowboy boots are her art form. She writes, "Representation of American Flags in Western boot design is overwhelmingly masculine. Women primarily sewed both flags and boot tops while being denied full boot making knowledge. I honor American heroes Harriet Tubman, Soujourner Truth, Ida B. Wells, Ona Judge, Susan B. Anthony, Sacajawea, and every unrecognized woman sewing through history. The crossed needles reference Civil War sabres, the bootstraps reference Martin Luther King: 'it is a cruel jest to say to a bootless man that he ought to lift himself by his own bootstraps.' Building boots as a woman is resistance to counter American racism and misogyny with symbols of national pride." Saboteuse Bespoke, *Flags of Our Foremothers*, American, 2022. Collection of Sarah Madeleine T. Guerin.

WELLS

Fig. 3: This pair of bespoke boots was made for Canadian country-western star, Orville Peck by boot maker Emily Boksenbaum. Her work complements Peck's unapologetic persona and bold interpretation of the Western aesthetic. Underhill Studio, *In the Dead of Night You Say it's Time to Ride*, American, 2024. Collection of Orville Peck.

TIME TO RIDE

Fig. 4: Heath Ledger
and Jake Gyllenhaal in
Brokeback Mountain, 2005.

Fig. 5: Lil Nas X in the music video for *Old Town Road*, 2019.

teaching the many students who flock to her for training.

Lisa Sorrell, one of the most famous bespoke boot makers today, was inspired to become a cowboy boot maker after seeing an article about McGuffin. Born in Missouri, Sorrell learned to sew at a young age, and after moving to Guthrie, Oklahoma, in 1990, she began to sew boot uppers for Jay Griffith. Within short order she wanted to expand her skills and learn boot making, but there was some resistance, so she left Griffith. She then apprenticed with Ray Dorwart, a former student of Griffith's. Under Dorwart, Sorrell honed her skills and eventually launched her own shop, specializing in custom cowboy boots distinguished by intricate inlay and overlay designs. Each pair she makes is named after a song that has inspired her (fig. 1). Sorrell also shares her deep knowledge of the craft through her books and online video series and, like boot makers before her, has begun taking apprentices.

Sorrell's first apprentice was Flora Knight. A talented maker and musician, Knight reached out to Sorrell with the idea that she wanted to learn cowboy boot making. Sorrell accepted her, and Knight relocated from Canada to Guthrie. Like Sorrell, Knight's intricate work reveals a deep understanding of traditional design and construction. After Knight completed her time with Sorrell, she returned home to Canada, where she continues to make bespoke boots.

Living in Lynn, Massachusetts, once the historic center of shoemaking in America, Sarah Madeleine T. Guerin struggled to find anyone to teach her to make boots. Eventually, however, she found Jim Covington, a respected cowboy boot maker with lineage going back to Texas through Ed Martin and Randy Merrell, who was working within traveling distance. At first Guerin was focused on shoemaking, but she soon realized that cowboy boot making was her true calling. In 2012 she launched her own workshop, seeing her work on cowboy boots as part of a long lineage of handmade footwear in Lynn. Under Ray Dorwart, she further honed her skills, developing a style distinguished by intricate inlay and overlay, bold compositions, and a keen eye for historical details. Though geographically removed from the traditional centers of cowboy boot making, Guerin sees this distance as a source of freedom. She has been able to develop her own style outside of regional expectations, while still paying deep respect to the traditions of the craft. One of her signature details is the incorporation of hand embroidery into every pair of boots she makes, an element that adds a personal and often narrative-driven touch to her work (fig. 2). Like other master boot makers, Guerin is also a dedicated educator and advocate for handcraft, teaching shoemaking at the Rhode Island School of Design in Providence.

Emily Boksenbaum, based in Boulder, Colorado, first learned shoemaking at Brooklyn Shoe Space before training under Deana McGuffin. She has since gone on to develop many of her own methods and techniques, using leather to translate her unique artwork into wearable footwear. Boksenbaum opened her studio, UnderHill Leather Studio, in 2019. The name reflects both the street where the brand began and a commitment to honoring nature.[93] A principal value for Boksenbaum is a commitment to sustainable practices to minimize waste in her production (fig. 3). One of her many clients has been musician Orville Peck. His unique stage persona, unabashed sexuality, and bold interpretation of the Western aesthetic align with Boksenbaum's fusion of tradition and contemporary artistry.

THE RIGHT ATTITUDE

If the answer to who should be making cowboy boots was changing, so too was the answer to who should be "allowed" to wear them. By the turn of the twenty-first century, cowboy boots had been integrated into fashion but, for some, this proved frustrating. Those who fretted often repeated the idea that "cowboy is an attitude, a mind-set. It's a return to a simpler time."[94] What this meant, however, was unclear. What defined this "attitude," and what was meant by "a simpler time"? The events of September 11th, 2001 pressed this "attitude" into service.

Right before entering the presidential race in 1999, George W. Bush purchased a ranch in Texas and made a point of being seen working in cowboy clothes, including boots, despite not being a horseback rider.[95] This continued after he won the election. Bush regularly wore cowboy boots and hats in Washington, but the visibility of these sartorial choices became more pronounced after 9/11, when American patriotism came to the fore.[96] It was not only Bush's clothing that reflected his Americanness—his responses to the tragedy were also discussed in cowboy terms. His quick reaction to label Iran, Iraq, and North Korea as the "axis of evil" and his initiation of the US-led global "war on terror" were seen by many in the international community as "cowboy diplomacy," which reinforced the idea "that the US can rely only on itself."[97] While the world saw this as a criticism, conservatives argued that rather than being insulting, these comments were badges of honor: "The cowboy spirit, which is alive and well in America and anathema to the Axis countries and others who hate us, is characterized by freedom: that cliché that was born of good reason, rugged individualism. The cowboy cherishes freedom above all else, as do most Americans."[98] For many, Bush had the right "attitude" to be wearing cowboy boots.

FREEDOM

As the 2000s continued, more people sought to express their freedom by wearing cowboy boots. Movies and media continued to influence sales. One Western apparel shop owner said in 2006 that the cowboy boot market was "like a roller coaster gathering speed when boot-centric movies like *The Dukes of Hazzard*, *Walk the Line*, and *Brokeback Mountain* come out."[99] It is not surprising that the shop owner mentioned *Brokeback Mountain* (fig. 4). The 2005 film won a Golden Globe award and was "showing remarkable success in conservative, red-state towns and cities" despite the controversy it courted—it centered on a pair of male ranch hands who develop a complicated physical and emotional relationship.[100] It was one of the most talked about films of the decade but remained highly controversial. Comments criticizing the film were plentiful, with many trying to suggest that the characters were not "real" cowboys. "Those two young men who had the hots for each other in 'Brokeback Mountain' were not cowboys, they were sheepherders. . . . Ask any real cattleman. Do not ask a dude with lizard skin boots and designer jeans," wrote one disgruntled commentator.[101] His use of "lizard skin boots" to suggest that the "dude" mentioned was not a "real" cowboy reflected the increasing concern about who should be "allowed" to wear cowboy boots, who had the right "attitude" to wear them.

These were, in fact, coded terms. The decades of mythmaking concerning the cowboy and the Wild West had made him one-dimensional. The cowboy was White, male, heteronormative, embracing freedom yet living by his own rules, which conveniently always coincided with "traditional values." Indeed, *Brokeback Mountain* challenged little of this stereotype with the exception of its representation of homosexuality. The movie's controversy was further stoked when country music superstar Willie Nelson released a cover of the 1981 song "Cowboys Are Frequently, Secretly Fond of Each Other" by Ned Sublette the following year, paying homage to gay cowboys and asking what people really thought "them boots and saddles was all

BANS OFF
OUR BODIE

Fig. 6: In 2020, Canadian footwear designer Aurora James designed this pair of cowboy boots after the US Supreme Court overturned *Roe vs. Wade* for her "My Body My Choice" collection. Brother Vellies, *My Body My Choice*, American-designed, Mexican-made, 2023.

TEXAS
USA
TEXAS
USA

Fig. 7, opposite: The Louis Vuitton LV Texan on the runway at the Menswear Fall/Winter 2024–2025 show as part of Paris Fashion Week on January 16, 2024.

Fig. 8: Studio portrait of a cowboy, early 20th century.

about?" Scholars and activists rushed in to illuminate the "forgotten culture of exclusively masculine, sometimes erotic, and often intimate camaraderie" of the Wild West. This line of inquiry made some uncomfortable, as it highlighted the tension between the constructed myth of the "real" cowboy and the reclamation of the actual history of cowboys, which challenged long-held assumptions about masculinity and tradition in American culture.

YEEHAW AGENDA

In hindsight, it might seem that concerns about sexual identity were at the center of the controversy surrounding Lil Nas X's hit trap country song "Old Town Road" when it came out in 2018, but it was his race, not his sexual orientation, which he did not reveal until the following year, that caused a stir.[102] The song, which mixed country and trap musical traditions, went viral on TikTok, and when remixed with the addition of country singer Billy Ray Cyrus, it eventually became the longest-running *Billboard* No. 1 song in history (fig. 5). Not only was the music extremely popular, but the fact that Lil Nas X was dressing the part also grabbed attention. Journalist Claudia Miller wrote that "Chart-topping 'Old Town Road' sensation Lil Nas X already won Musical Event of the Year for his remix with Billy Ray Cyrus, but the real event was his choice of footwear. He rocked a cowboy-chic look with a tall hat, fringed shirt, and chaps sewn onto his jeans. He completed the ensemble with a pair of classic black leather cowboy boots that featured intricate patterns and exposed stitching."[103]

Lil Nas X became central to the Yeehaw Agenda, a term created by influencer Bri Malandro, that was motivated by the desire to reclaim the history of the impact of Black culture on America. It emphasized inclusivity through the embrace of the cowboy aesthetic as a way to challenge outdated stereotypes and embrace a broader spectrum of experiences and identities. The removal of "Old Town Road" from *Billboard*'s Hot Country Songs chart in 2019 because it did not meet the "traditional" criteria for a country song only added fuel to the fire about who was "allowed" to participate in and define country and western culture.

An article in *Esquire*, "The 'Yeehaw Agenda' Has Been Here for Years. We're Just Finally Paying Attention,"[104] noted that "In positioning 'Old Town Road' as somehow lacking the hallmarks of country music, *Billboard* (whether intentionally or not), aligned itself with a complex history of musical stratification along racial lines. The resulting furor over the song's classification forced many to come to terms with the whitewashing of Western aesthetics and how that reality had influenced Black erasure in popular culture."[105]

REDRESSED

A number of Black fashion designers sought to address this whitewashing as well and began integrating cowboy boots into their shows and offerings. Fashion designer Kerby Jean-Raymond, founder of Pyer Moss, looked to the Black cowboys of the nineteenth century—specifically Bill Pickett, one of the first rodeo stars of the era—and paired his clothing with cowboy boot–referencing footwear as well as sneakers from his new Reebok collaboration for his F18 collection. His campaign "American, Also" included images of Black riders from the Compton Cowboys and the rodeo team Cowgirls of Color, shining a spotlight on Black riders. However, Black cowboys were given even greater visibility when many rode in Black Lives Matter protests around the country.

In 2020, Canadian footwear designer Aurora James, who had collaborated with Kerby Jean-Raymond and founded her own footwear and accessories brand,

Fig. 9: Cover of *act ii: Cowboy Carter* by Beyoncé, 2024.

COWBOY CARTER

Fig. 10: As cowboy boots and their meanings were shifting in the United States, *botas picudas* emerged in northern Mexico in the early 2000s. This pair features only slightly extended toes. Mexican, mid-2000s.

Fig. 11: Tribaleros from Matehuala wearing *botas picudas*. Edith Valle, 21st century.

Brother Vellies, turned to cowboy boots in reaction to the Supreme Court ruling that overturned *Roe v. Wade*. For her "My Body My Choice" collection, she reimagined her Doodle Boots, leveraging the long history of the incorporation of narrative into the design of cowboy boots, and launched the boots on International Women's Day in 2023 (fig. 6).

COWBOY FASHION

Perhaps one of the most pointed reclamations of the Western aesthetic in fashion was Pharrell Williams's Fall/Winter 2024 collection for Louis Vuitton—his second collection for the house—for which he chose the Wild West as inspiration, delving deep into the cultural complexity and diversity of nineteenth-century America to highlight the impact of Black, Indigenous, and Mexican influence on Western fashion to reimagine what contemporary American luxury could look like and who should wear it. Williams worked with luxury cowboy boot brand Stallion Boots, established by Pedro Muñoz in El Paso, Texas, in 1980, as well as Louis Vuitton's own Rochambeau Ranch, which is located in Alvarado, Texas, right outside of Dallas–Fort Worth, where many of the brand's leather accessories have been produced since 2019.

Of the styles offered in the collection, the most traditional was the LV Texan (fig. 7). It featured stamping and overlay work, which included depictions of cacti, scorpions, and bluebonnets. "Texas, USA," was written along the collar of the boots, and the LV initials, very traditionally, were placed in the center of the shaft. When asked about the collection, Williams said, "I felt like when you see cowboys portrayed, you see only a few versions. You never really get to see what some of the original cowboys really look like. They look like us, they look like me. They look Black, they look Native American" (fig. 8). The rest of the collection sought to uphold this vision as Williams also worked with Lakȟóta and Dakȟóta makers.

BACKLASH

The same could not be said about Beyoncé and her use of the cowboy aesthetic when she released her 2024 album, *Cowboy Carter* (fig. 9). Lucchese, name-checked in her music, embraced the attention from a fellow Texan and her fans. However, many critics—some overtly racist—dismissed her interpretation of Western aesthetics, questioning her place in country music and cowboy culture. Her embrace of Western iconography included cowboy hats, leather fringe, spurred heels, and, like Pharrell Williams's work, challenged the idea that the cowboy, long mythologized as rugged, masculine, and White, was never just one thing. Her rhinestone costuming also directly references the history of country-western music traditions that, as Beyoncé makes clear in *Cowboy Carter*, owe a debt to the many Black musicians central to the creation of the genre.

RESISTANCE

A number of Indigenous artists have long confronted the intertwined legacies of colonialism and the cowboy in their work. Cree artist Kent Monkman often references footwear—both Western and Indigenous—in his paintings and sculptural installations. Kiowa beadwork artist Teri Greeves, however, works directly with footwear, building on the long-standing tradition of embellishing shoes and moccasins in many Indigenous nations. In her piece *Deer Woman as Lady Luck*, Greeves beads iconic Western motifs such as dice and playing cards alongside a depiction of Deer Woman, a figure who is half human and half deer. The entire work is a study in cultural fusion and symbolic transformation. The substrate—a pair of high-heeled sneakers—is beaded with cowboy boot motifs, interrupted only by the central figure who straddles two worlds: human and animal, traditional and contemporary.

Anishinaabe artist Barry Ace's sculptural assemblages often incorporate his signature use of electronic components and glass bead medicine flower motifs to draw parallels to the colonial histories of Canada through material and metaphor. In his 2023 piece *Gwiiwzens Dreamed of Spirit Horses*, discarded electronic wires echo trail dusters and symbolize the erasure of the Ojibwe Spirit Horse, a breed nearly driven to extinction in the last century. The inclusion of children's cowboy boots speaks to hope for the future and the dream of the return of these horses.

BOTAS PICUDAS

As cowboy boots and their meanings shifted in the United States in the 2000s, a new relationship between boots and performance developed in Mexico. *Botas picudas*, or "pointy boots," emerged in the early 2000s in northern Mexico as central elements of *tribal guarachero*, also called 3Ball (fig. 10), a music and dance movement that blended precontact rhythms, cumbia, and electronic beats as a form of cultural reclamation.[106]

Botas picudas were directly related to the dance competitions in *tribal guarachero* clubs, where groups of young men competed doing high-energy, synchronized routines in coordinating outfits, including boots. The longer and more dramatic the toes, the more impressive the performance. At first, the dancers made their own boots, but eventually boot makers in small towns across Mexico began specializing in custom *botas picudas*, crafting ever more extreme designs (fig. 11).

Some saw this as a passing fad, but *botas picudas* gained mainstream recognition in the 2010s when the movement grew across Mexico and into the United States, particularly in Texas. *Botas picudas* became a declaration of group identity and merged deep cultural heritage with contemporary expression. In many ways, these *bota picudas* and the collective dancing that they were made for shared the same emphasis on the spirit of cooperation expressed by charros and Mexican rodeo traditions, rather than the focus on individual achievement seen in the United States.[107] These divergent meanings and uses of the cowboy boot reflect just how much cultural context impacts the evolution of style and identity.

MYTH AS A MIRROR

Cowboy boots have never been just footwear—they have always been reflections of the world in which they were worn (figs. 12, 13, and 14). They have symbolized labor, freedom, individualism, nationalism, race, gender, morality, success, fashion, and politics—the list goes on. They have been used to tell truths and have also been used to craft myths. Today, as competing visions of America wrestle for dominance, the cowboy and his boots are once again being invoked—sometimes as symbols of inclusive progress, sometimes as emblems of the past. Yet history makes one thing clear: Cowboys have never belonged to just one story, one ideology, or one group of people. The same is true of their boots. From the cattle trails to concert stages, from Hollywood back lots to the White House lawn, cowboy boots have been endlessly shaped and reshaped to reflect the world in which they are worn.

Fig. 12: The fine art of leather tooling is on full display with this pair of Lucchese *Kents*. Lucchese, American, 21st century.

Fig. 13: Using the warm brown leather of the upper to create a sense of landscape, the maker of this pair of boots added cacti to the boot tops to situate them in the West and hung a cow skull, like the sun, in the middle of the shaft to complete the vision. San Diego Boots, Mexican, 1990s. Collected by Stephen Pitch, generous gift of Anna Savoy.

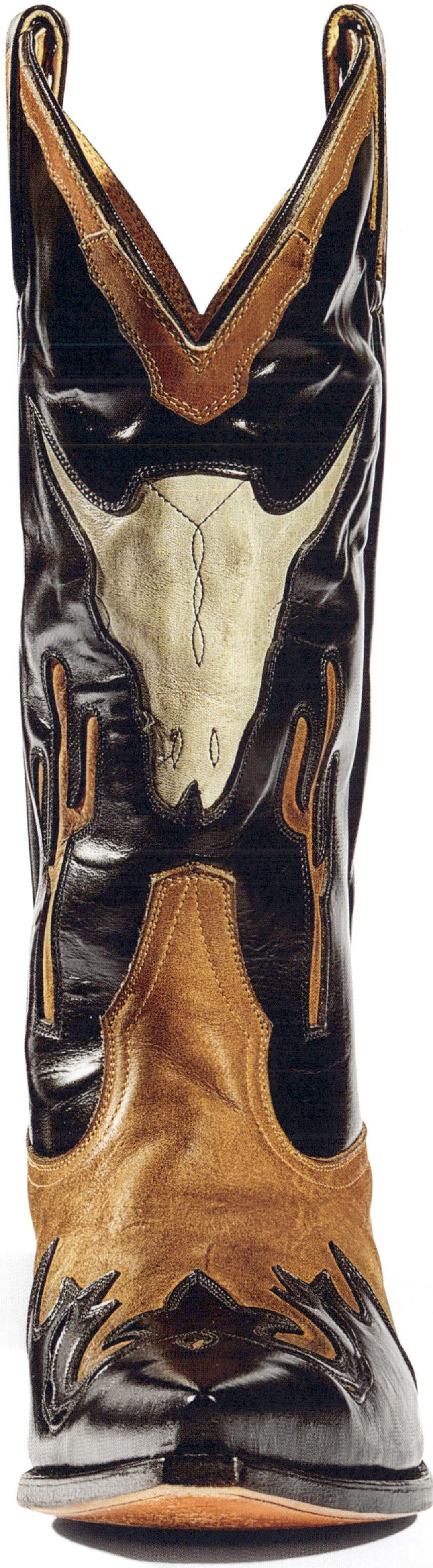

T
C

Fig. 14: This pair of Tiffany-blue alligator cowboy boots features sterling silver details and was made by Arditti for a New York heiress. Arditti, American, 2010.

KEEP ON THE SUNNY SIDE
EDDY ARNOLD
CATTLE CALL

INTERVIEW WITH MASTER BOOT MAKER LISA SORRELL

ELIZABETH SEMMELHACK: How did you get into cowboy boot making?

LISA SORRELL: I was raised in a really conservative little church where the women all wore long hair and long dresses, and my mom started teaching me to sew at age twelve. By the time I was fifteen, I was sewing clothing professionally. I remember one of the first bits of instruction she gave me: She sat me down with the sewing machine and she touched the tension wheel, and she said, This is the tension wheel. Don't ever touch it. When I was twenty, my husband and I married and moved to Guthrie, Oklahoma, and after six months, I got bored and I answered an ad in the paper for stitching boot tops. I had no idea what that meant. I had also never worn cowboy boots.

ES: These first boots, were they stitched only, or did they also have inlay and overlay, techniques that you are now famous for?

LS: It was just stitching. I still have the practice piece of leather that I stitched on to apply for that job. It is terrible—just a one-row stitch pattern. But I was really fortunate in that I was working for a man named Jay Griffith. He had a big order he was working on and he was also making boots for a bronc rider who was trying to start his own line of boots. He just needed me to do very simple one-row stitch patterns. I would come into work and there would be piles of boot tops to stitch, and they were all one row. I could not have asked for better training because I just sat there doing one-row stitch patterns over and over. That taught me how to control the machine. I wanted to do a good job, but it wasn't super important as there weren't multiple rows.

ES: Do you remember the first time you did inlay work?

LS: I don't remember the first time, but I do remember doing inlay work. Jay let me make a pair of tops for myself that he would finish. I remember making those because I didn't skive [thin down the edges of leather where it will be joined to reduce bulk] anything. Jay came back with the boot tops to tell me, but I'd already glued everything in place. He just said, No, you have to skive them. So I had to try to skive them with everything glued in place, which was a good lesson, I guess.

ES: When did you go from sewing boot tops to building boots?

LS: I had already figured out after being at Jay's for maybe six months that I wanted to be a boot maker. I finally left Jay after a year and a half because I couldn't cash my paychecks.

ES: Why did you want to be a boot maker?

LS: I liked it because the one thing I didn't like about sewing clothing was that it was a "girl" thing. I was expected to do it because I was a girl, and that offended me. When I found boot making, I realized, I sewed and could do pretty designs in nice colors, *but* also there's physical labor involved—I loved that. So I decided that I wanted to be a boot maker. I remember sitting at my sewing machine and making these calculations—it's probably going to take me this many years to get all the machines I need, and I've got to get somebody to train me. It'll probably be seven years before I can have my own shop. I think I accomplished it in five.

ES: That is very impressive. Were your clients men or women or both?

LS: Mostly men. After I left Jay, I knew that if I left the industry, I'd never get back in. It just wouldn't happen. So I began stitching tops independently for boot makers across the country. That was my way. We bought a sewing machine and cleared out the laundry room, and that was my little work area. I stitched tops, and I did that for about three years until we could afford to pay someone to train me. That person was Ray Dorwart, who worked here in Guthrie.

ES: What was it like then moving to boot building? Making a pair of fully lasted boots?

LS: I don't really remember the process of learning to do multiple rows of stitching or inlay. I've been doing stitching for so long that my sewing machine is practically an extension of my body. But learning to build boots was hard. There is absolutely nothing about cowboy boots that's intuitive. I worked with Ray for a year and a half, and I still remember I would be in my shop after I left him, and I'd have to go look at my notebook to figure out what came next, because cowboy boots are hard and they're physical. I pushed myself really too hard because I felt like I had to do everything that men were doing, and I was smaller and weaker, and I had two young children, and I pushed my body too hard. I'm paying for it now, but that's the way it goes.

ES: Do you still have the first pair of boots that you made?

LS: Yes, I do. When I took my class with Ray, I made two pairs of boots, one for myself and one for my husband. I don't remember which one I made first. Neither one of them fit, but I do still have both. Boot making is a challenge in all sorts of ways. You can make a really beautiful boot that doesn't fit, or make a boot that fits, but the customer doesn't like the colors after all, and there are multiple ways for it to go wrong.

ES: So now you make only bespoke boots, correct? How many boots a year are you able—or maybe *willing* is a better way of putting it—to produce?

LS: "Willing to produce" is probably the question, because several years ago I started a business selling leather tools and supplies to other shoemakers. This has absolutely taken over my life. I really enjoy it because within boot making, we've been telling each other that we have to get young people into this trade so it will survive. But we took our eyes off the suppliers—there's one factory in the entire world left that makes wooden shoe pegs. So it's a really scary time, and most of my energy now goes to the supplies business. Making boots is a treat and a pleasure for me, but I probably only make six pairs a year now. I've also branched out into making shoes, which I'm not very good at it yet, but it's super fun. I also probably make six to ten pairs of shoes a year. They go a little faster.

ES: Tell me more about these shoes.

LS: I'm making cowboy boot shoes. In the 1940s, Olsen-Stelzer started making shoes on a cowboy boot last because leather was scarce due to the war. I've always been absolutely obsessed with those shoes. They had carved uppers, or quarters. I don't know how to do carving, so I thought it'd be fun to do inlay and overlay on the quarters, and they have been pretty popular. I really enjoy wearing them. When women see them, they want to wear them, but I've also made a couple of pairs for men, including a pair for a private chef in Washington, DC. He wanted vegetables on his shoes, but not just any vegetables. He wanted summer vegetables. That was a challenge—the asparagus and carrots. . . .

ES: I've worked a lot on men and sneakers and have noticed that it is at their feet that many men are willing to take their greatest sartorial risk. They will wear very colorful sneakers, but the rest of what they are wearing is quite subdued. It seems that something similar happens with men and cowboy boots.

LS: I always say that cowboy boots are a way for men to wear high heels and bright colors.

ES: So how far are some customers willing to go with extravagant design?

LS: It completely depends on the person. Some of them just want it wild and others want it very plain. And then others do want it wild, but only on the boot tops, where it's hidden.

ES: Why do people hide the most decorative part of cowboy boots under their pant legs?

LS: I tell my customers that the art on cowboy boot tops is like lingerie. It's there and you feel pretty, but not everyone gets to see it. Some people like that little hidden bit of something special. Others sometimes want a bright color on the foot such as a wingtip or something that suggests that there is something more going on with the boots. You also see guys who will tuck their jeans into their boots, so there is a big variety of how people want to wear their boots and have them seen.

ES: I find it so curious that people will wear elaborate boots but not really want to show them off. There also seems to be sensitivity about who should be wearing cowboy boots. Recently I was watching a person on TikTok talking about how uncomfortable he is that so many people are wearing cowboy boots. For him, he feels that when a person puts on a pair of cowboy boots, they are agreeing to a set of principles—moral principles. Is this sensitivity about who should and shouldn't wear cowboy boots real?

LS: There are some strong feelings about it, but here's the thing, and it's a part of history that real cowboys perhaps might not know—the original cowboy boots were gear. Cowboy boots are just a type of footwear. If you're six-foot-tall and you want to wear red pumps, go for it. I don't care. It's a shoe. If you want to wear cowboy boots and you're a lawyer in DC, wear them. They're footwear.

I've been going through old catalogues to try to discover the history of the cowboy boot, and what I'm seeing is that they develop bright colors and colorful designs as they moved into the entertainment industry. Obviously you don't have to have flowers and butterflies on your boot tops to ride them on horse, right? So cowboy boots became associated with entertainment very early on, and they have never lost this association. It is historically accurate to wear them for fun, for entertainment. Cowboy boots have never exclusively been a working shoe.

1 William Taylor et al., “The Origins of Saddles and Riding Technology in East Asia: Discoveries from the Mongolian Altai,” *Antiquity* 98, no. 397 (Cambridge University Press, 2024): 102–118. See also Richard Dibon-Smith, “The Stirrup as Revolutionary Device,” in *New Ideas About the Past: Seven Essays in Cultural History* (Berkeley and Los Angeles: University of California Press, 1989): 103–10.

2 Elizabeth Semmelhack, *Standing Tall: The Curious History of Men in Heels* (Bata Shoe Museum, 2015): 12.

3 As these imported horses spread north through conflict, cultural exchange, and breakaway feral herds, many Indigenous nations across North America actively embraced them. Over the centuries, cowboy culture and Indigenous cultures would intertwine in complex ways.

4 Allan Greer, *Property and Dispossession: Natives, Empires, and Land in Early Modern North America* (Cambridge University Press, 2018): 129.

5 Greer, *Property and Dispossession*, 111.

6 Lawrence Clayton, Jim Hoy, Jerald Underwood, *Vaqueros, Cowboys, and Buckaroos* (University of Texas Press, 2010): 8.

7 Andrew Sluyter, *Black Ranching Frontiers: African Cattle Herders of the Atlantic World, 1500–1900* (Yale University Press, 2012): np.

8 Sluyter, *Black Ranching Frontiers*, 55.

9 Sluyter, *Black Ranching Frontiers*, 56.

10 David Dary, *Cowboy Culture: A Saga of Five Centuries* (University of Kansas Press, 1989): 14.

11 The unique charro culture that emerged in Mexico and America is beyond the scope of this book. For more information, see Laura R. Barraclough, *Charros: How Mexican Cowboys Are Remapping Race and American Identity* (University of California Press, 2019).

12 Martha Zierden, “Exploring the Cattle Economy of Colonial South Carolina,” *The Charleston Museum*, July 2020, https://www.charlestonmuseum.org.

13 Federal Writers’ Project, *When I Was a Slave: Memoirs from the Slave Narrative Collection* (Dover Publications, 2002).

14 Charles Dickens, ed., *Household Words: A Weekly Journal*, vol. XI, no. 254 (1855): 348.

15 *The Young Elocutionist, No. 1* (A.L. Bancroft & Co., 1882), 47.

16 Slavery had played a central role in the creation of the independent Texas Republic. In direct contravention of Mexican law, US citizens brought significant numbers of enslaved people into the region in an effort to establish ranching and cotton cultivation. Ensuring the right to own slaves was central to the rebellion. The right to uphold the “peculiar institution,” as it was euphemistically termed, was also a point of tension when the Republic was annexed by the United States in 1860. In the early nineteenth century, US immigrants to the Mexican state of Coahuila y Tejas brought significant numbers of enslaved people into the region, directly violating Mexican law. These settlers aimed to establish ranching and cotton cultivation using slave labor. This was one of the factors that led to the Texas Revolution and the creation of the independent Republic of Texas in 1836. When Texas became a US state in 1845, slavery remained a contentious issue, but the practice continued unabated. The state entered the Union with around 30,000 enslaved people. Near the start of the war in 1860, the state’s enslaved population had grown to 182,566 men, women, and children. The state also counted between three and five million cattle. These figures would shape the rise of the cowboy in the post–Civil War era.

17 Despite the fact that the majority of slaves were ill shod, the brogan market was significant and was a boon to the shoe manufacturers in the North. A British report in 1854 notes this: “No inconsiderable quantity of the coarser kind of shoes called ‘brogans’ is disposed of for the use of slaves in the south . . . the northern manufacturers . . . have little reason to wish for a speedy termination of slavery.” “Things as They Are in America,” *Chambers’s Journal of Popular Literature, Science and Art* (Lowell, MA), no. 25 (June 24, 1854): 390.

18 Some Southerners were desperate to make shoemaking a more local industry, a point in part reflected in the high sale price given to slaves with shoemaking skills. Former slave Cicely Cawthon recounted that the first slave her “master” had was a shoemaker. “They paid big money for him . . . He was ’bout as valuable as the blacksmith. I do not remember how much they paid for him, but it was big money.” Despite these attempts footwear production remained a Northern monopoly, and once the Civil War broke out the want of footwear was felt keenly throughout the South.

19 Harold S. Wilson, *Confederate Industry: Manufacturers and Quartermasters in the Civil War* (University Press of Mississippi, 2002), 85.

20 For an in-depth look at this time see: Christopher Knowlton, *Cattle Kingdom: The Hidden History of the Cowboy West* (Houghton Mifflin Harcourt, 2017).

21 Steven D. Dortch, “Chisholm Trail,” *The Encyclopedia of Oklahoma History and Culture*, https://www.okhistory.org/publications/encyclopediaonline.

22 It has been suggested that because so many cowboys from Texas were formally enslaved Blacks, the term *cowboy* came from the racist and demeaning use of the word *boy* when referring to adult Black men. This is a compelling insight, especially given the increased tensions around race, particularly in the South at the time the cattle drives began pointing them North. However, since the term was used and embraced by many White cowboys as well, both in autobiographical texts and in the popular media, more research needs to be done on the origin of the word.

23 “Reminiscences of,” *Miles City Independent*, July 18, 1919, 8.

24 Barbara Brackman, “Legend Posing as History: Hyer, Justin, and the Origin of the Cowboy Boot,” *Kansas History: A Journal of the Central Plains* 18, no. 1 (1995): 41.

25 *The Cosmopolitan*, December 1886, 222.

26 Emerson Hough, *America of the Americans or The Builders of the Nation: The Cowboy I* (America of the Americans Society Publishers, 1897), 53.

27 *Our Great West: A Study of the Present Conditions and Future Possibilities of the New Commonwealths and Capitals of the United States* (1893).

28 Knowlton, *Cattle Kingdom*, 36.

29 “American West: The Cattle Industry,” *History on the Net*, https://www.historyonthenet.com.

30 Brackman, “Legend Posing as History: Hyer, Justin, and the Origin of the Cowboy Boot,” *Kansas History: A Journal of the Central Plains* 18, no. 1 (1995): 35.

31 Brackman, “Legend Posing as History,” 36.

32 “With the ‘Cowboys’ in Wyoming,” *Puck* XVI, no. 404 (1884): 219.

33 David Edwin Harrell, Edwin S. Gaustad, John B. Boles, and Sally Foreman Griffth, *Unto a Good Land: A History of the American People, Volume 2: From 1865*, (Eerdman, 2005), 575.

34 Dominic Erdozain, *One Nation Under Guns: How Gun Culture Distorts Our History and Threatens Our Democracy* (Crown, 2024), 88.

35 Harry Coods and Jas. R. Marie, “Pawnees,” in “Leases of Lands in Indian Territory,” in *Reports of Committees of the Senate of the United States for the First Session of the Forty-Ninth Congress, 1885–86, Senate Documents*, vol. 5 (US Government Printing Office, 1885–1886), 577.

36 Brackman, “Legend Posing as History,” 35.

37 “John W. Cubine Obituary,” *Confederate Veteran Magazine*, June, 1911.

38 Brackman, “Legend Posing as History,” 43.

39 Brackman, “Legend Posing as History,” 44.

40 Brackman, “Legend Posing as History,” 44.

41 Stephen Aron, “History of the American West Gets a Much-Needed Rewrite,” *Smithsonian Magazine*, (2016) https://www.smithsonianmag.com.

42 PBS, “Buffalo Bill,” *The West*, accessed March 4, 2025, http://www.pbs.org.

43 *United States Department of Labor, Descriptions of Occupations: Boots and Shoes, Harness and Saddlery, Tanning* (Government Printing Office, 1918), 25.

44 Thanks is given to Sarah Madeleine T. Guerin for bringing this shoe to my attention.

45 “Discard High Heel: Changed Conditions on Western Plains Cause Cowboy to Alter Regalia,” *L’abeille de la Nouvelle-Orleans*, September 21, 1909, 6.

46 “Rodeo Education,” *ProRodeo Hall of Fame*, https://www.prorodeohalloffame.com.

47 Hough, *The Cowboy*, 53.

48 Edwin Legrand Sabin, *Bar B Boys: Or, The Young Cow-Punchers* (Thomas Y. Crowell, 1909), 243.

49 C. R. Rasmussen, *A Dictionary of Footwear* (The Sanford Press, 1912), 24.

50 Willa Cather, *My Ántonia* (Houghton Mifflin Company, 1954), 13. Originally published 1918.

51 Tyler Beard, *Art of the Boot* (Gibbs Smith, 1999), 78.

52 Beard, *Art of the Boot*, 78.

53 “Go West, Young Dude, Go West: Where Ranch Life Provides New Delights in the Lines of Riding, Roping, and Round-ups,” *Vogue*, June 15, 1928, 45.

54 “Go West,” *Vogue*.

55 “Go West,” *Vogue*.

56 Deborah B. Shepherd, “The 1939–1940 New York World’s Fair: Typical American Families Build Tomorrow.” (2011). University of Mary Washington. Student Research Submissions, 23.

57 Shepherd, “The 1939–1940 New York World’s Fair,” 19.

58 Myriad sources give his age as ranging from six to ten. See: “When Bootmaker’s Art Becomes a Song,” *The Hour*, December 15, 1976, 49.

59 Edward Loya, “Ray Jones: Texas’s Greatest Bootmaker?” *Illume Connect*, October 12, 2021, https://illumeconnect.com.

60 Loya, “Ray Jones.”

61 Loya, “Ray Jones.”

62 Loya, “Ray Jones.”

63 J. Frank Dobie, *The Voice of the Coyote* (Little, Brown and Company, 1949), 6.
64 Ernie Pyle, "The Roving Reporter," *The Toledo News-Bee*, March 10, 1938, 17.
65 Robbin Coons, "Autry Makes Friends in Spite of Gaudy Clothes," *St. Joseph News-Press*, October 8, 1939, 10A.
66 "Roy Rogers," *Herald-Journal*, December 7, 1941, 4D.
67 Robert W. Phillips, *Roy Rogers: A Biography, Radio History, Television Career Chronicle, Discography, Filmography, Comicography, Merchandising and Advertising History, Collectibles Description, Bibliography and Index* (McFarland, 1995), 30.
68 "Texas Glamor Girls Are Rodeo Stars," *Life*, October 1939, 60.
69 Milton Harker, "Cowboy Film Star Cherishes Gift from Dying Boy," *The Youngstown Daily Vindicator*, Saturday, December 24, 1938, 17.
70 Oliver Jensen, "Hopalong Hits the Jackpot," *Life*, June 12, 1950, 63.
71 "The Duel of Honor," *The Rifleman*, Episode 7, 1958.
72 Barry Miles, *Hippie* (Sterling Publishing, 2003), 30.
73 Susan Gallagher, "Dudes Find Western Duds Fashionable, Comfortable," *The Bulletin*, January 28, 1978, np.
74 Gallagher, "Dudes Find Western Duds Fashionable."
75 "Psychologists Evaluate 'American Uniform,'" *The Tuscaloosa News*, September 16, 1979, 16C.
76 William W. Savage Jr., "The Cowboy Myth," *The Cowboy: Six-Shooters, Songs and Sex*, edited by Charles W. Harris and Buck Rainey (University of Oklahoma Press, 1975), 157.
77 "Cowboy Boots' Popularity Grows," *The Spokesman-Review*, December 26, 1976, 26.
78 "Cowboy Boots' Popularity Grows," 26.
79 Priscilla Tucker, "Sixties Flash on 59th Street," *New York Magazine*, March 28, 1977.
80 Aaron Latham, "The Ballad of the Urban Cowboy: America's Search for True Grit," *Esquire*, September 12, 1978, https://classic.esquire.com.
81 William K. Stevens, "The Urban Cowboy: 1978 Style," *The New York Times*, June 20, 1978.
82 Nishi Bassi, *Dressed to Impress* (Bata Shoe Museum, 2024), 5.
83 "Anteaters Get the Boot," *New York Magazine*, March 8, 1982, 10.
84 "Anteaters," *New York Magazine*.
85 William K. Stevens, "The Urban Cowboy."
86 "Tailored for President?" *The Washington Post, Times Herald (1959-1973);* September 24, 1967.
87 Donnie Radcliffe, "First Cowboy: Reagan's $1,000 Boots," *The Washington Post*, September 3, 1981.
88 "Olsen-Stelzer Making a Comeback," *The Clay County Leader*, August 24, 2006, 1 and 3.
89 "Most Expensive Cowboy Boots," *Forbes*, April 4, 2006, https://www.forbes.com.
90 Beard, *Art of the Boot*, 66.
91 Beard, *Art of the Boot*, 66.
92 "Deana McGuffin's Roots in Teaching Folks to Make Custom Cowboy Boots," posted January 5, 2023, by Jermiah Craig, YouTube, 3 min., 8 sec., https://www.youtube.com/watch?v=QHJQctiAH00.
93 UnderHill Leather Studio, https://www.underhillleather.com/about.
94 Jim Jones, "A New Version of the Bible Testifies to Cowboy's Faith," *The Victoria Advocate*, September 10, 2000, 9F.
95 David A. Smith, *Cowboy Presidents: The Frontier Myth and U.S. Politics Since 1900* (University of Oklahoma Press, 2021), 189.
96 Smith, *Cowboy Presidents*, 190.
97 William Schneider, "Cowboy Diplomacy," *The Atlantic*, March 1, 2002, https://www.theatlantic.com.
98 Kathleen Parker, "The Cowboy Spirit Is Alive and Kicking Up Its Heels in America," *The Hour*, June 2, 2002.
99 Madeleine Marr, "Good Leather Boots Comfortable, Stylish All Year Long," *The Free Lance-Star*, Fredericksburg, Virgina, February 5, 2006, F6.
100 Peter Wallsten, "President Steers Clear of 'Brokeback Mountain,'" *Lawrence Journal-World*, January 24, 2006, 4A.
101 Keith LaDouceur, "Chick Flicks," *Ocala Star-Banner*, March 15, 2006, 4B.
102 Lil Nas X did not reveal his sexual orientation until the following year.
103 Claudia Miller, "8 Best Boots at the CMA Awards 2019," *Footwear News*, November 13, 2019, https://www.yahoo.com/lifestyle/.
104 Stephanie Smith-Strickland, "The 'Yeehaw' Agenda Has Been Here for Years, We're Just Finally Paying Attention," *Esquire*, November 4, 2019, https://www.esquire.com.
105 Strickland, "The 'Yeehaw' Agenda."
106 For an in-depth study, see, Helena Simonett and Cesar Burgos Davila, "Mexican Pointy Boots and the Tribal Scene: Global Appropriations of Local Cultural Practices in the Virtual Age," *Transatlantica* 1 (2015), accessed March 4, 2025, https://doi.org/10.4000/transatlantica.7596.
107 For an in-depth look see: Laura R. Barraclough, *Charros: How Mexican Cowboys are Remapping Race and American Identity* (University of California Press, 2019).

FRINGE, FLORALS, AND BUCKSKIN

1 Ted J. Brasser, "Native American Clothing: An Illustrated History," *Native American Clothing: An Illustrated History* (Firefly Books, 2009).
2 Laurel Wilson, "American Cowboy Dress: Function to Fashion," *Dress* 28, no. 1 (January 2001): 40, https://doi.org/10.1179/036121101805297680.
3 Wilson, 40–41.
4 Adolph Hungry Wolf, *Traditional Dress: Knowledge and Methods of Old-Time Clothings* (Book Publishing Co., 1990), 80.
5 Hungry Wolf, *Traditional Dress*, 80.
6 Wilson, "American Cowboy Dress," 40.
7 E. J. W. Barber, *Prehistoric Textiles: The Development of Cloth in the Neolithic and Bronze Ages with Special Reference to the Aegean* (Princeton University Press, 1991), 83, http://archive.org/details/prehistorictexti0000barb_d8p7.
8 Turtle Island is a name used by the Indigenous community when referring to what is now known as North America. The term is rooted in Anishinaabe and Haudenosaunee creation stories honoring Indigenous cosmologies and ontologies.
9 Darren R. Préfontaine, "Norway House/Norway House Style," in *kôhkominawak ocihcîwâwa – Our Grandmothers' Hands: Repatriating Métis Material* (Gabriel Dumont Institute Press, 2023), 20.
10 Sherry Farrell Racette, "Sewing Ourselves Together: Clothing, Decorative Arts and the Expression of Metis and Half Breed Identity," August 1, 2004, 64, http://hdl.handle.net/1993/3304.
11 James A. Hanson, "Laced Coats and Leather Jackets: The Great Plains Intercultural Clothing Exchange," in *Plains Indian Studies: A Collection of Essays in Honor of John C. Ewers and Waldo R. Wedel* (Smithsonian Institution Press, 1982), 109.
12 The Métis are one of three Indigenous groups recognized under Section 35 of the Canadian Constitution, alongside First Nations and Inuit peoples. Métis peoples emerged from relations between First Nations women and European men during the Fur Trade era and adopted a distinct culture, language, and way of life. The descendants of these relations comprise the present-day Métis Nation and occupy territories spanning Alberta, Saskatchewan and Manitoba, as well as regions in Ontario, British Columbia, the Northwest Territories and the Northern United States.
13 Hanson, "Laced Coats," 111.
14 Tasha Hubbard, "'The Buffaloes Are Gone' or 'Return: Buffalo'? - The Relationship of the Buffalo to Indigenous Creative Expression," *The Canadian Journal of Native Studies* 29, no. 1/2 (2009): 69.
15 Bill Ashcroft, Gareth Griffiths, and Helen Tiffin, *Post-Colonial Studies: The Key Concepts*, 3rd ed. (Routledge, 2013), https://doi.org/10.4324/978023777855.
16 Hanson, "Laced Coats," 109.

RALPH LAUREN AND THE MYTH OF THE WEST

1 William E. Guest, "Ralph Lauren: Three Purveyors of Executive Style," *The New York Times Magazine*, September 8, 1985, https://www.nytimes.com/1985/09/08/magazine/ralph-lauren-three-purveyors-of-executive-style.html.
2 Woody Hochswender, "Fashion: on the Urban Frontier, Clothes Reflect the Spirit of the West," *The New York Times Magazine*, April 9, 1989, https://www.nytimes.com/1989/04/09/style/fashion-on-the-urban-frontier-clothes-reflect-the-spirit-of-the-west.html.
3 Paul L. Underwood, "On the Heels of History," *RL Mag*, https://www.ralphlauren.co.uk/en/rlmag/rrl-boots-made-in-texas.html.

This book is published on the occasion of the exhibition *Rough and Ready: A History of the Cowboy Boot*, organized by the Bata Shoe Museum in Toronto, Canada: May 7, 2025–October 2026

The Bata Shoe Museum Foundation and Elizabeth Semmelhack extend our sincerest thanks to Charles Miers and Margaret Chace at Rizzoli, our editor Loren Olson, and designer, Sarco, who gave beautiful expression to cowboy boot aesthetics. Special thanks are due to Lee Miller, Lisa Sorrell and Jaime Nudie. We also thank Carrlyn Miller and the team at Texas Traditions, Tony Benattar, Sarah Madeleine T. Guerin, Flora Knight, Orville Peck, Adam Goeglein, Tomasso Arditti, Charlie Neuenschwander, the Autry Museum of the American West, and the Glenbow. Lastly we give special thanks to Nishi Bassi, Justine Woods, Alexandra Geropoulos, and Ada Hopkins as well as the entire Bata Shoe Museum team. We also wish to thank photographers Rachael Reid and Kailee Mandel.

BATA SHOE MUSEUM

First published in
the United States of America
in 2026 by Rizzoli Electa
A Division of Rizzoli
International Publications, Inc.
49 West 27th Street, 4th Floor
New York, NY 10001
rizzoliusa.com

Publisher: Charles Miers
Associate Publisher: Margaret Chace
Senior Editor: Loren Olson
Copy Editor: Kelli Rae Patton
Production Manager: Barbara Sadick
Design: Sarco

2026 2027 2028 2029 / 10 9 8 7 6 5 4 3 2 1

Printed in Hong Kong
ISBN: 978-0-8478-7416-3
Library of Congress Control Number: 2025945842

Facebook.com/RizzoliNewYork
Instagram.com/RizzoliBooks
Pinterest.com/RizzoliBooks
Youtube.com/user/RizzoliNY

The authorized representative in the EU for product safety and compliance is Mondadori Libri S.p.A., via Gian Battista Vico 42, Milan, Italy, 20123
www.mondadori.it

Cover: Inlaid cowboy boots, c. 1950.
Endpapers: Assembling a cowboy boot in Alpine, Texas, Russell Lee, 1939.
Full title: Stewart-Romero cowboy boot, early 1940s.
Table of contents: Men's bolo tie, 1950s.
Introduction: Painting of a cowboy, Walter M. Baumhofer, c. 1930s-1940s.
p. 8: *This Man was Once a Cowboy*, Russell Lee, 1940.
p. 56: *Buffalo Bill's Wild West: A Bucking Bronco*, c. 1885.
p. 108: Lee Miller in his workshop, 2019.
p. 114: Gene Autry with Champion the Wonder Horse, c. 1950.
p. 160: Nocona Boots advertisement, Alex Ebel, 1980s.
p. 206: Lil Nas X photographed by Kelia Anne and styled by Hodo Musa.
p. 234: Lisa Sorrell in her workshop, 2025.
p. 237: Cowboy boots made by Lisa Sorrell, 2025.

PHOTOGRAPHY CREDITS:

Album/Alamy Stock Photo: p. 13; Archive Photos/Getty Images: pp. 143, 158; Arthur Elgort, Conde Nast Archives via Getty Images: pp. 202, 204–205; Associated Press, AP Photo: p. 168; Bata Shoe Museum: pp. 52, 54, 160, 169; Bata Shoe Museum/Kailee Mandel: contents page, pp. 10–11, 18–19, 38–39, 42–43, 84–85, 94–95, 140–141, 146–147, 162, 164–165, 184–185, 188–189, 194–195, 196–197, 200–201, 218–219, 228–229, 230–231; Bata Shoe Museum/Rachael Reid: title page, pp. 22–23, 24–25, 34–35, 36–37, 40–41, 44–45, 47, 60–61, 62 (top), 71, 78–79, 80–81, 82, 88–89, 90–91, 96–97, 98–99, 100–101, 102–103, 104–105, 106–107, 118–119, 122–123, 124–125, 126–127, 130–131, 134–135, 136–137, 138–139, 144–145, 148–149, 152, 154–155, 179–171, 172–173, 176–177, 182–183, 187, 190–191, 192–193, 198–199, 208–209, 210–211, 224–225; Bata Shoe Museum/Ron Wood: p. 14; Bettmann/Getty Images: pp. 55, 117; Bill Manns/Shutterstock: introduction page; Bridgeman Images: p. 21; Buyenlarge/Getty Images: p. 29; C. E. Fry/Buyenlarge/Getty Images: pp. 53, 56; Camerique/Alamy Stock Photo: p. 77; Charlie Neuenschwander: pp. 234, 237; Cinematic/Alamy Stock Photo: p. 142; Columbia Records: p. 216; Dell Publishing/Getty Images: p. 128; Edith Valle: p. 226; Entertainment Pictures /Alamy Stock Photo: p. 174; Everett Collection Inc./Alamy Stock Photo: p. 129; Glasshouse Images/Alamy Stock Photo: pp. 68–69; The Glenbow: pp. 74–75; H. Armstrong Roberts/Classicstock/Getty Images: p. 116; Henry Diltz - Corbis via Getty Images: p. 153; Hi-Story/Alamy Stock Photo: p. 32; Hulton Archive/Getty Images: pp. 120, 166–167; Hyer Boots Archives: pp. 66, 121; Jasper Graham: pp. 212–213; Kansas State Historical Society: p. 92; Lebrecht History/Bridgeman Images: p. 49; Marion Post Wolcott/Getty Images: p. 83; Metropolitan Museum of Art: p. 12; Michael Ochs Archives/Getty Images: pp. 132, 133, 159; Morphy Auctions: p. 67; Nat Geo Image Collection: p. 76; NGS Image Collection: pp. 72–73; North Wind Picture Archives/Alamy Stock Photo: p. 48; Paramount Pictures/Archive Photos/Getty Images: p. 179; Penta Springs Limited/Alamy Stock Photo: p. 17; Peter Newark American Pictures/Bridgeman Images: pp. 33, 51; Pictorial Press Ltd./Alamy Stock Photo: p. 156; PictureLux/The Hollywood Archive/Alamy Photos: p. 163; Piemags/Alamy Stock Photo: p. 15; Sarah Madeleine T. Guerin: p. 63; Screen Archives/Getty Images: p. 114; Silver Screen Collection/Getty Images: pp. 150–151; Smithsonian National Museum of African American History and Culture: p. 221; Stephane Cardinale - Corbis via Getty Images: p. 220; Steven Visneau Photography: p. 108; Stocktrek Images, Inc./Alamy Stock Photo: p. 59; Swim Ink 2 LLC/Getty Images: p. 70; TCD/Prod.DB/Alamy Stock Photo: pp. 214–215; Three Lions/Getty Images: p. 86; Tony Lama Archives: p. 93; Transcendental Graphics/Getty Images: pp. 28, 30–31; Tribune Content Agency LLC/Alamy Stock Photo: pp. 222–223; UC Berkeley, Bancroft Library via Online Archive of California: p. 16; University of North Texas Special Collections: pp. 87, 159; US Library of Congress: pp. 8, 26, 27, 62, 64–65; US Library of Congress/Russell Lee: pp. 110, 111, 112.

Unless otherwise specified, all artifacts in this book are in the Bata Shoe Museum Collection.

FSC
www.fsc.org
MIX
Paper | Supporting responsible forestry
FSC™ C023053

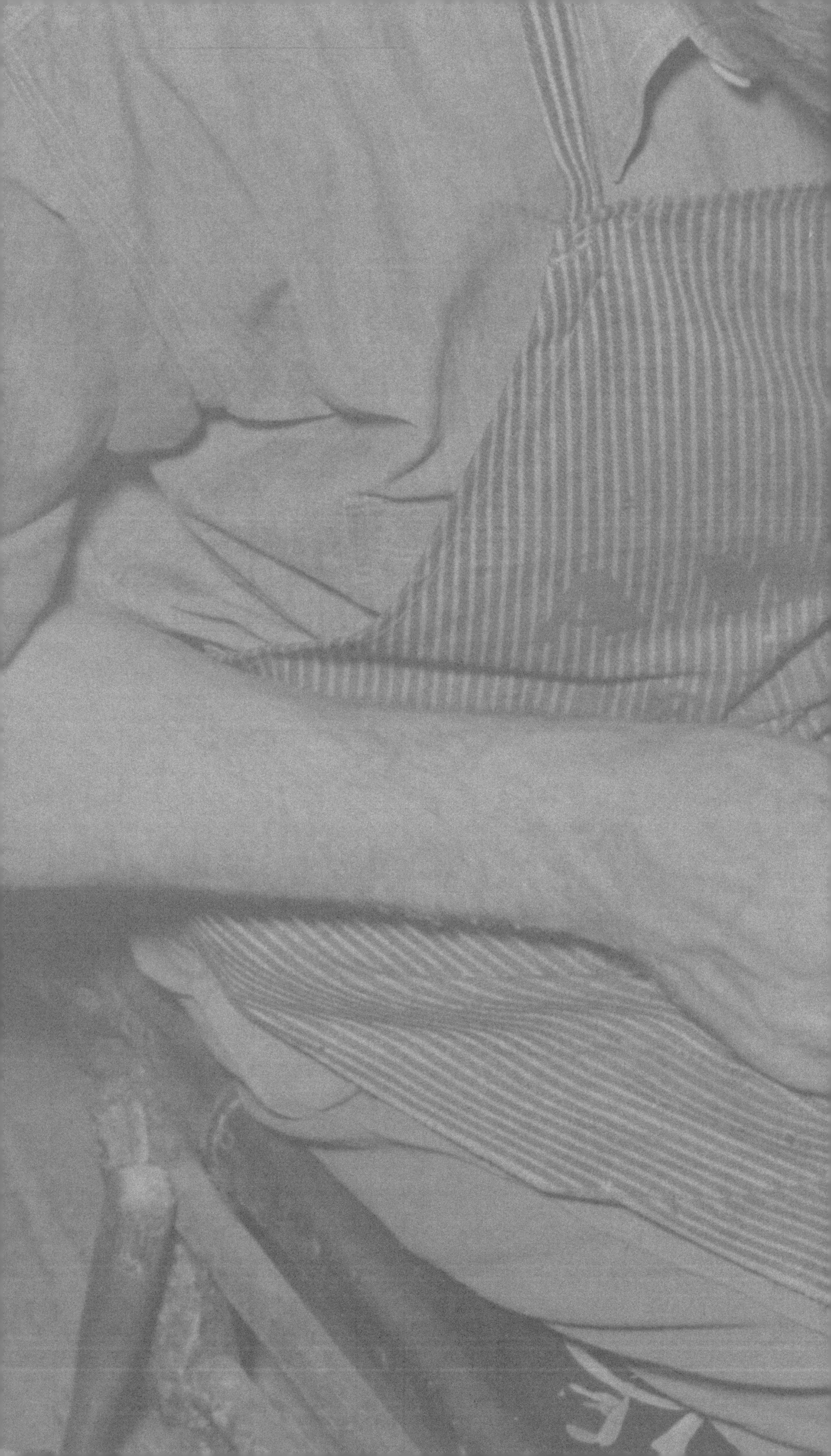